Yard Buildings

Yard Buildings

A Home Owner's Bible

MEL MARSHALL

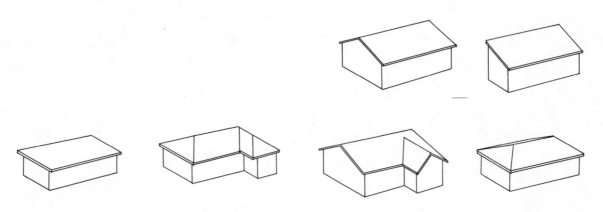

DOUBLEDAY & COMPANY, INC., GARDEN CITY, NEW YORK

1981

ACKNOWLEDGMENTS

For assistance in providing and checking data, furnishing materials used in photographs, and other courtesies, thanks go to Herman Stuller of Foxworth-Gailbreath Lumber Co., Price T. Smith Builders, James Kidd of Northeast Lumber Manufacturers Association, and Melvin L. Harmon of C F & I Steel Corporation.
Special thanks go also to Jess Roan for his rendering of architectural plans and the detail sketches.

Library of Congress Cataloging in Publication Data

Marshall, Mel.
  Yard buildings.

  1. Garden structures—Design and construction—
Amateurs' manuals.   2. Building—Amateurs' manuals.
I. Title.
TH4961.M37   690'.89

ISBN: 0-385-15400-3
Library of Congress Catalog Card Number 80–1125

CONTENTS

CHAPTER ONE

What This Book Is About

Obviously, it's about yard buildings, those small convenient structures that fill a multitude of needs in their many forms, yet can be erected single-handedly or with a minimum of help.

Most yard buildings are well within the scope of the amateur do-it-yourself builder. Most of them are inexpensive to put up, even in a day of inflated prices. For the most part, they call for a knowledge of just basic building skills, and a minimum of tools.

This book gives you the information you'll need to put up your own all-purpose or special-purpose yard buildings. Preliminary chapters provide data that can be applied to all kinds of yard buildings, such as lists of the tools you'll require, what their use is, why they will be needed, and how to use them to best advantage. These chapters also detail basic procedures common to all building projects, definitions of builders' terms, step-by-step descriptions of key operations, and a discussion of the materials you'll encounter.

These preliminaries are followed by individual chapters containing detailed plans for more than a dozen small structures designed to provide additional facilities for storage space, hobby work, or recreation, or simply to add to your pleasure in living and entertaining.

More and more, people viewing what promises to be an energy-poor future begin to think in terms of expanding family recreation facilities. The expansion might be a hobby room or game room, an outdoor dining shelter, or a poolside lounge. It might be something more practical: a workshop, a playhouse for the youngsters, a garage or shelter for a boat or dune buggy, or secure storage for seldom-used items that are now cluttering up house closets or a garage suddenly inadequate to house the power mower and garden tools and what cross-country moving men classify as "miscellaneous clutter."

Yard buildings are the answer in many cases. Usually they're the most economical and satisfactory solution to filling any of the needs just mentioned and a few more that might have been overlooked. All the plans in later chapters fill one or more of those needs, and most of the plans can be modified to serve one purpose today, another tomorrow. All the plans have been drawn so that they can be followed easily, even if you've never looked at a building plan before. Technical data, wherever possible, are given in nontechnical terms. Each chapter describing a building gives you complete details of any special construction features that are not covered in the preliminary chapters on building basics.

It doesn't matter if you have little or no experience with tools. Using tools calls for skills that can be acquired in a relatively short time; in fact, *using* tools is really the only way to *learn* to use them. If there is a secret to learning building skills, that secret is practicing these skills and profiting by your errors. And a secondary purpose of this book is to reduce to the barest minimum the number of errors you're likely to make.

An old Chinese saying is that a journey of ten thousand miles begins with a single step. That saying applies to building as well as traveling. Less effort and time are required for learning to use builders' tools adequately than for learning to wield a tennis racket or a set of golf clubs. You can become a reasonably skilled builder much more quickly than you can learn to turn in consistent golf scores in the low eighties.

We are, of course, living in a do-it-yourself era. Though building costs have risen and will rise higher as inflation continues, professional builders still have more jobs than they can handle, more demands for their time than there are hours in a working day. Contractors who once welcomed small jobs—such as yard buildings—to tide them over between big jobs now go from one major building project to the next. The individual who wants a small yard building at an affordable price finds that the best—and often the only—way to get one is to put it up himself.

Right about now you may be asking yourself, "Why bother to build something from scratch when there are so many prefabricated yard buildings that I can buy ready to bolt together?"

That's a fair question and it deserves an honest answer. You may, if your need is for an exceedingly elementary structure, such as a storage shed for garden tools or something similar, be very well served by a prefab building. However, honesty requires that the answer be complete. Prefabs have drawbacks. Most of them have ceilings of less than 6′, so it may be difficult to stand erect inside them. They tend to be something less than weatherproof. Most importantly, prefabs will seldom give you exactly the features you require to suit a special personal need. And some prefabs are so complicated to assemble that you might as well build your own and get exactly what you want instead of a compromise building that won't satisfy you.

Let's explore this last item. If you want a yard building for a special purpose, you're not likely to find one on the prefab market. A workshop, for example, should have width, length, and ceiling height sufficient for a woodworking hobbyist to turn a sheet of 4′ × 8′ panelboard easily, and to store both boards and panelboards off the floor, but still have easy access to them. There are a few prefab yard buildings with enough square footage of floor space to meet this requirement, but none I have seen provide adequate ceiling height. And a prefabricated yard building of the size we're looking for now will cost as much as the shell of a workshop you build from scratch, which will have its floor space laid out to suit your precise needs.

Or let's say that you want a yard building designed to get the family hobbies out of the house, where they'll be out of the way of everyday living

routines. The only way you're apt to find such a building is to put it up yourself, following a plan drawn to provide what you need in the way of storage areas and other facilities. If you set out to modify a prefab, you'll quickly discover that you've taken on a difficult and costly job, for a majority of prefabs are designed with presized metal wall sections bolted together. It's extremely difficult to add interior features such as cabinet work, shelving, and so on to buildings of this type. It's also more costly than building what you need and want.

Suiting individual requirements in a nation of individualists has been the goal I kept in mind constantly while preparing the plans in later chapters of this book. Without exception, these plans give you one or more options for modification. And the options aren't afterthoughts, they're part of the plans themselves.

There's another area of freedom the plans give you: the widest possible choice of exterior materials as well as interior finish and trim. About the only commonly used material you won't find is the thin sheet metal typical of prefabs. For economy as well as workability and saving time, the plans favor lumber, plywood, and the man-made hardboards. Quite often you'll want to match in a yard building the exterior finish of your house, and this is relatively easy to do with modern panelboards as well as with V-groove, lap, and other hardboard sidings.

On the other hand, if matching your home's exterior is less important to you than economy of construction, each list of materials gives you options, specifying the quantity needed of each type of finish listed. Armed with this information, you can quickly find out how the cost of one type of material compares with others.

Because yard buildings are predominantly owner-built and because few owner-builders are professionals, construction features have been kept as simple as possible, and few of the buildings call for specialized tools or extraordinary skills. Incidentally, when studying the plans in later chapters, don't overlook the possibilities that some of them offer in using existing walls and structures. For example, if you have a detached garage, you might decide to connect the garage to your house by simply building two walls between house and garage and turning the new area into a building that has the features you want for a workshop or hobby room or recreation room. Then, using the garage plans in Chapter Six, you can build yourself a new garage.

Pitfalls that may be encountered are also noted in the text that accompanies the plans. Knowing what *not* to do is often as important as knowing what *to* do. And since this business of avoiding pitfalls has come up, let's follow up by noting a few that apply to any building project you might undertake.

One pitfall you may encounter, if you're not well acquainted with building materials, involves the difference in the methods used to price lumber and panelboards. Lumber—and that term itself will be elaborated a bit further along—is sold by the *board foot*. This is a unit of *volume*. Panelboards, including plywood, are sold by the square foot, which is a unit of *area*. There is a difference between the number of square feet of wall surface that a given number of board feet of lumber 6″, 8″, 10″, and 12″ wide will cover. Usually, the greatest economy can be achieved by using the *widest* possible boards to cover a given number of square feet of area. And, as lumber is generally quoted in terms of board feet, this easily results in confusion as to whether boards or panelboards are the most economical. To help you unscrew this inscrutable building trade practice, you'll find tables in Appendix A that give the square foot coverage in terms of boards of different widths.

As a general rule, the types of materials listed as first choice in the chapters that follow will be those that are the most economical on a nationwide average. In cases where a specific material, higher in cost than some others, is recommended, the reasons are always given so that you can weigh all factors involved.

Often, materials will be recommended because of the amount of time they save in handling, or because use of a certain type of material eliminates the need for some traditional building practice. For instance, traditional structures have for generations relied on bracing and bulk to provide structural rigidity and wind resistance. Modern sheet materials often can be used with fewer structural members to deliver the same rigidity and resistance to natural forces.

There are a few potential pitfalls that need to be looked at while you are doing the very first planning for the yard building you have in mind. One of these is the situation in your home neighborhood with respect to building codes. By all means visit your city hall or county courthouse and find out as much as you can about building code requirements even before you begin to plan.

These codes vary widely from one area to another, from city to city and county to county. Some areas have municipal building codes but no county codes; in places where both exist, their provisions don't always agree. Generally speaking, rural areas relatively distant from large cities tend to give you the widest freedom of choice. This is especially true of rural areas that have not yet been faced with the problem of speculative builders, some of whom will cut corners if not restrained by codes.

In places where the owner-builder is the rule rather than the exception, governing authorities seem to take the attitude that only a fool will put up a substandard building if it is to be used by himself and his family. In such places, the backyard builder is left pretty much to his own devices. However, most of us have encountered stories in the news media that tell of children's playhouses, tree houses, even doghouses, being condemned because prior approval of their plans was not obtained. In some cases the actual buildings have been safe and carefully constructed. Some have even exceeded building code standards, but have been ordered torn down because their builders failed to get plans approved.

Public safety and health dictate the building code sections that are usually most restrictive. These are the parts dealing with wiring and plumbing. Faulty wiring can cause injury, even death, from electrical shock or fire. Faulty plumbing can endanger your own or your neighbor's health by the uncontrolled discharge of effluents. No matter how confident you are of your ability, those in charge of enforcing building codes won't take your word that you know what you're doing.

Almost anywhere you live you can just about count on one of three code requirements, even if all you're putting up is a yard building. The most stringent will require that a licensed electrician and plumber do the entire electrical and plumbing installations. Less strict codes require that the wiring and plumbing you do yourself be connected to the main power source by a licensed electrician, and that plumbing be joined to the mains by a licensed plumber. The least restrictive codes merely call for inspection of your work by a plumber or electrician holding a journeyman license. Be sure to check your local requirements early in your planning.

Another potential pitfall lies in choosing the site of your yard building. The size of your lot isn't as important as the ground contours and the type of soil. If your land has high or low spots, steep rises or falls, or if the soil is either loose and sandy or clayey and impermeable, give thought to drainage before making your final choice of a site, as well as to the foundation you will put under your yard building.

Again we go back to general rules. In most cases where the surface is very irregular or sloping, a lot of leveling or filling might run up your labor time and costs. In sandy, loose soil, you will want to choose a solid perimeter footing; in heavy impermeable soils, a post foundation will be more satisfactory. But, on land that has a pronounced slope, a solid perimeter foundation may act as a dam, backing up water as it runs off. This requires an excessively high floor line to keep the inside of your building from becoming a lake. In such a case, a post foundation is indicated to allow for drainage.

If you're not sure of rainfall figures for the area in which you live, the nearest office of the National Weather Service can provide them. This same office can give you the depth of the frost line, which will dictate how deep you must go with your foundation to avoid damage by the freezing and thawing of the ground. Remember that foundation depths indicated in the plans given here are based on *averages,* not on specific local conditions. You may find it necessary to go deeper than the plans indicate.

Finally, if you modify any of the plans given in the chapters that follow, be sure to make a new plan that includes the modifications. Don't try to keep changes in your mind. Be sure also to change the bills of material when you change your plans. Nothing is more frustrating on a Saturday or Sunday afternoon than to arrive at a point in your building where you need something you've forgotten to order. Finding yourself short of a few boards or lacking that final sheet of panelboard needed to complete the job does nothing to improve your temper.

Make up a tentative work schedule before you begin, and consult your building supply house to find out what materials, if any, are in short supply or must be ordered well in advance. Doing this bit of preliminary paper work will enable you to get an orderly flow of material as you need it.

All these advance precautions might seem to be a lot of trouble, perhaps you even consider them time wasted. They aren't. If you're like most weekend builders, your chief interest is in seeing your job move ahead smoothly. Preliminary planning enables you to do this.

Each of the pitfalls noted is very real. Avoid them all, and your work will move ahead smoothly and satisfactorily.

CHAPTER TWO

Tools and Materials

Let's start this chapter with three assumptions.

One: You now own no tools except the three most common ones found in households where until now no one has been interested in developing do-it-yourself building skills. These three tools are a nondescript hammer, a screwdriver, and slip-joint pliers.

Two: You want to buy only the tools that are essential to the work you plan to do, in order to hold your investment to a minimum.

Three: You know almost as little about building materials as you do about tools, and need information about virtually all the sizes of boards, panelboards, nails, and so on.

From the point of these assumptions we can move on to square two, with a tool list stripped down to your basic needs. Some of the tools on the list may not seem essential to you. Please be patient. Reasons why you'll need them will appear. So will reasons why some tools you might think you'll need aren't included on the list of basics.

POWER TOOLS

Today, powered hand tools are basic and have never been as plentiful or as affordable. While other prices have risen between the 1970s and the 1980s, prices for powered hand tools have in most cases gone down. This is especially true of the three essential items. In the late 1960s and early 1970s, a 7¼″ circular saw cost around $40; today such saws are universally priced in the $30 range. Electric drills were a bargain in that same period at $30; now vastly improved models are in the $20–$25 range. Saber saws in the early

1970s were underpowered and limited in use, and priced at $25 or more. The saber saw of the 1980s is powerful, versatile, and available in the $20 price range.

Most powered hand tools now have accessories that help the beginner master the techniques of handling them easily and quickly. Learning to saw a straight line or form a well-fitted miter joint; to drill a hole; to cut odd shapes and angles are no problem for the average newcomer to powered hand tools.

First item on the tool list is a 7¼″ circular saw. If you're thinking that you've never used portable power tools, and you're weighing the cost of a saw of this kind against the admittedly lower cost of a handsaw, it might surprise you that it's far easier to learn to use the former than the latter. Ask any carpenter and he'll confirm this. All sorts of saw line guides can be bought or rigged up to enable you to saw completely straight lines, but sawing a true line with a handsaw is a skill that takes time to acquire. In addition, a portable power saw reduces otherwise time-consuming building cuts to seconds.

Next, invest in a saber saw, often incorrectly called a jigsaw. If you want to be precise in nomenclature, a jigsaw is a bench tool, operating on its own table. Its nearest relative is a band saw, which is another bench tool. A saber saw is a lightweight tool that goes places where the bigger, heavier circular saw would be inconvenient and perhaps impossible to use.

A saber saw makes an easy job of irregular cuts such as arcs, circles, and zigzags, and also makes inside or pocket cuts, which involve taking

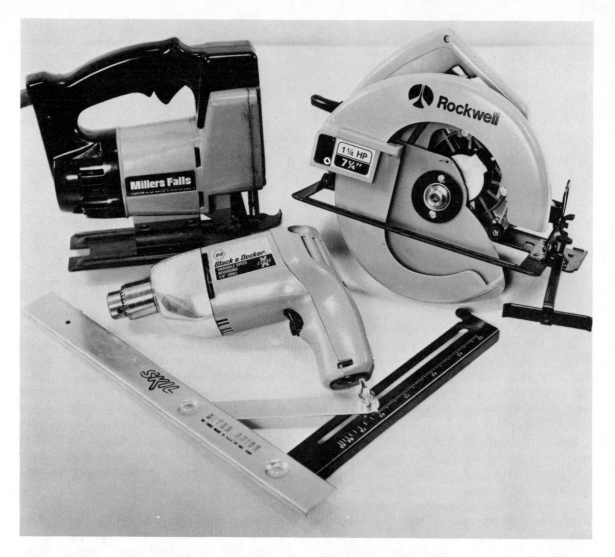

Fig. 1. **Here are the three essential power tools: a variable-speed saber saw, a variable-speed reversing ⅜″ drill, and a 7¼″ circular saw. Both saws accept rip-fences, as shown on the circular saw. The adjustable angle guide in the foreground can be used with any saw.**

a small square or rectangle out of the middle of a board or panel. Get a variable speed saber saw that's heavy enough to be guided easily. The variable speed feature allows you to start precise cuts at low blade speeds, then speed up the blade as the cut progresses. It also enables you to match blade speed to the thickness and type of material you're sawing.

Your third and last portable power tool is an electric drill. Choose a ⅜″ drill rather than the less costly ¼″ size, which is favored by many beginning craftsmen. Assuming again that you're totally unfamiliar with tools, the "⅜″" and "¼″"

refer to the maximum size of the bits a drill will accept. The designations also provide a frame of reference to the power of the drill's motor; a ⅜″ drill will have a bit more power than a ¼″ drill, and a ½″ drill will be fitted with a more powerful motor than a ⅜″ type.

For all practical purposes, a ⅜″ drill will be adequate for any job you're likely to run into as an amateur builder. A ½″ drill is a professional's tool, used in heavy, repetitive jobs such as drilling through concrete and making holes with a hole saw to accommodate pipe and conduit runs through the framing timbers of a building. Do get a drill that has both variable speed and reversing features. These add very little to the tool's cost and make it much easier to use and more versatile.

These three are the only portable tools you'll need for the average small building job. This is being written during an inflationary period, so price estimates may not hold up, but by shopping around a bit you should be able to buy all three of these tools for about $75. You'll need to add a few dollars to your investment for blades and drill bits. Get a combination blade, a fine-cut blade, and a tungsten carbide-tipped blade for the circular saw; an assortment of fine, coarse, and metal-cutting blades for the saber saw, and an assortment of drill bits. A set of hole-cutters for the drill is a good investment. So is a sawing guide, which adjusts to any angle you might need to cut.

When shopping for portable power tools, don't make the mistake of buying bargain basement tools produced by unfamiliar makers. The four major manufacturers of portable power tools, Black & Decker, Millers Falls, Rockwell, and Skil, all produce tools that will give you excellent service. All these firms have nationwide service facilities that make it easy to get replacement

Fig. 2. **Basic hand tools, from bottom: a 10-point crosscut saw, a ¾″ chisel, a locking-jaws pliers, a solid-frame hacksaw, either a rip hammer (left) or a claw hammer, a portable vise, a pair of C-clamps, and a pry bar. Choose the style and weight hammer that feels best to you.**

parts or have repairs made. The difference between the tools produced by these makers is principally a matter of which tool by which manufacturer feels most comfortable in your hands. The differences in grip contour and balance might lead you to select a circular saw made by one, a saber saw from another, and a drill made by a third, but you can count on getting equally good performance from any tool made by any of these manufacturers.

HAND TOOLS

As for hand tools, the list of those needed may well be shorter than you've been anticipating. There are a lot of special-purpose tools on the market, designed to do one or two specific jobs superbly well and very quickly. You'll encounter few of these jobs in putting up yard buildings. Specialized tools are for building contractors who hire men to do specific jobs, and any time saved on these jobs means faster work and less expense per unit of completed work. Your need is for general-purpose tools that will do a lot of jobs satisfactorily, even though the time per job may be a few minutes longer.

Let's start with a hammer. Once more we come to a matter of personal "feel." There are two basic woodworking hammers, claw and rip (or

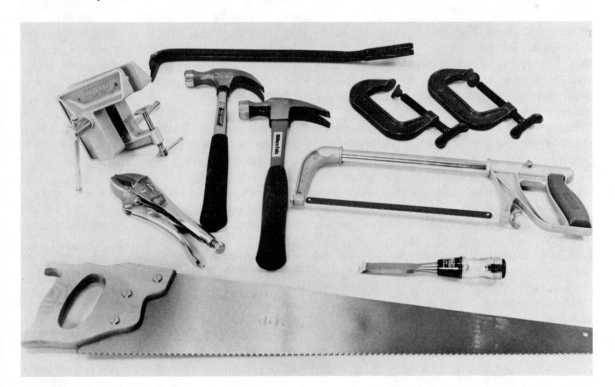

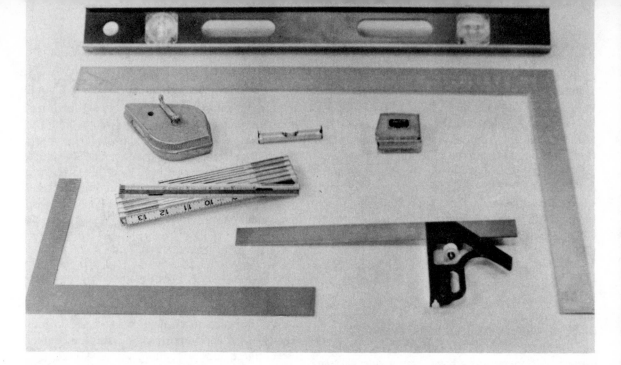

Fig. 3. **With the measuring devices shown here you can measure and mark any dimension required in normal construction. From the top: a spirit level, a large framing square, a chalk line, a line level, a steel tape, carpenter's folding rule, an adjustable square, and, as a handy but optional auxiliary, a small framing square that's handier in cramped quarters and on ladders than the full-sized square.**

framing) hammers. Fig. 2 shows the difference. You might like the balance of one kind better than you do that of the other. Whichever type you choose, get one heavy enough to drive big nails quickly, but not so heavy that its sheer weight will tire you to use it.

Buy a 10-point crosscut saw for the times when you'll be working in positions and places where a power saw can't be used. Fortunately, these positions and places are few. Usually, a handsaw will be used only to finish a cut that the power saws can't complete because their sole plates prevent the blade from moving those final few inches. The term "points" relates to the coarseness or fineness of the cut a saw makes: it is simply the number of teeth per inch of blade. The smaller the number of teeth, the coarser the cut will be. Don't bother buying a ripsaw. Ripping is easier with a power saw, and ripsaws are much less versatile than crosscut saws because of the difference in the shape and angle of the teeth.

Add a hacksaw to your tool list. Get the solid-frame kind, which hold blades more rigidly than do the break-frame type. You'll need a hacksaw for such jobs as sawing off the ends of anchor bolts, cutting reinforcing rods when putting down a concrete foundation or floor, and so on. Get a medium-coarse blade and a spare blade, for hacksaw blades do break occasionally.

For measuring, you'll need a 12′ steel tape, a framing square, and an adjustable square. You'll also need a spirit level at least 24″ long and a line level. A line level is handy, inexpensive, and time-saving; a line level is a small bubble in a metal case with hooks which allow it to be hung from a chalk line. You'll need a chalk line, too, for easy marking of long lines.

Only two more tools remain on your list. One is a good wood chisel, 1″ or 1½″ wide. If you feel flush, get a 1¼″ and a ¾″ chisel rather than just one. Sometimes you'll need to take off a little splinter of lumber in a place where a wide chisel can't reach. Finally, get a medium-duty pry bar, sometimes called a wrecking bar. If you make a mistake in nailing two boards together, a bar's the quickest and easiest way to get them apart without damaging the wood.

These are the tools you'll need for erecting the frame of a building and covering it. When you move on to the jobs that are involved in finishing the interior, you'll find two or three other items very handy.

High on the list is a miter box. You'll save money by getting a simple open-top miter box, which is basically a trough with precut grooves to guide the saw. With one of these, your crosscut saw can be used. Miter boxes which support the saw require a backsaw with a reinforced top edge, but this means buying both box and saw. For 90° and 45° cuts, the trough-shaped miter box is perfectly satisfactory. Both Stanley and Millers Falls make relatively inexpensive metal miter boxes which offer more versatility, but require a backsaw.

Locking-jaw pliers, the biggest size you can find, will prove to be a very handy tool. These pliers pull nails cleanly where a hammer or bar can't reach, and can be used as a vise or clamp. A pair of large C-clamps will provide you with the equivalent of another pair of hands. So will a small portable vise, the kind that attaches to a sawhorse.

Interior finish work, with paneling and molding, often requires accurately squared edges to make tight joints. To make the fine cuts necessary, use a block plane. For the most accurate work, it's often necessary to file edges or corners; for these jobs you'll need a medium-coarse wood rasp, a half-round mill bastard file, and a smooth-cut file. To sink nailheads below the surface so the holes can be filled with putty before painting, a nail set is used; get one small and one large size. None of the items on the hand tool list is very expensive. Costs range from $.30 or $.35 for the nail sets to about $8.00 for the miter box. A good hammer will cost about $6.00, a solid-frame hacksaw about $5.00, and the prices of the other items will range from a couple of bucks for a chalk line to $5.00 or $6.00 for chisels.

Fig. 4. **Interior finishing tools, from the top, counterclockwise: adjustable metal miter box, inexpensive wooden miter box that measures only 90° and 45° angles, block plane, small and large nail sets, a half-round mill bastard file, a smooth-cut file, and a fast-cutting Surform tool or, optionally, a medium-coarse wood rasp.**

All told, your investment in tools, including power tools, should be in the neighborhood of $150, and this would be the top figure. If you buy everything on the list, your total investment should be a bit less than that, if you take time to do a bit of shopping around.

There is one do-it-yourselfer's helper that's fairly expensive, but one that will save you enough time and effort to be a very worthwhile investment. This is the Black & Decker Workmate, a folding, portable workbench that incorporates a clamp the width of its top (Fig. 5).

Fig. 5. Especially if you're going to be working alone much of the time, the Workmate is an extremely handy and versatile helper. It will hold boards for sawing, drilling, planing, or filing, or will hold one board firmly in place while another is nailed to it. It's an optional choice, but you'll find it worth the rather substantial investment.

This tool will give you the equivalent of an extra pair of hands. The Workmate holds boards for sawing or joining, corners for fitting, it's an anchor for stock that must be drilled or shaped, and with some of its optional accessories it will give you a miniature workshop. It's a lot more than the king-size vise it appears to be at first glance, and if your budget allows for the purchase of one, you should give it serious consideration.

There is an alternative to making a major investment in tools if you're operating on a tight budget and don't plan to build anything beyond the yard building you're now planning. Check local rental agencies to see what they have available. Rental services have expanded greatly since their first appearance fifteen or twenty years ago. Even those in the smallest towns now rent such things as power saws, drills, and a pretty good assortment of hand tools.

You need to be conscious of the inconvenience

that might be experienced in renting tools, though. There will be occasions when you'll find yourself with an unexpected spare hour or two which could be devoted to an ongoing building project, but if you've been depending on rented tools you might find they're not readily available. But do check rental rates against the cost of the tools.

Should you decide to rent, try to make an arrangement to use the tools on a scheduled basis. Most agencies are very happy to cooperate with their customers who arrange for specific tools to be used for a definite period over weekends or days on the job. An arrangement for regular rental will solve the problem of availability and might be the basis for negotiating a lower rental rate.

As for using the tools on the list, the accompanying photos and their captions (Fig. 6 through Fig. 12) will do a better job of showing you this than could be done with words alone.

Fig. 6. While all good-quality circular saws have adjustments that allow you to saw at different angles, the adjustment you'll use most often is the one that raises and lowers the saw blade. The special plywood-cutting blade fitted to the saw shown should be set at a height that brings no more than 1/8″ of the tooth-points below the bottom side of the work.

Fig. 7. For most sawing, and especially for rip cuts, use a combination blade such as the one fitted to the saw shown, or a carbide-tipped blade. Carbide blades rarely need sharpening and will cut through nails without sustaining damage. Again, set the blade so that the tooth-points clear the bottom of the work by about 1/8″.

Fig. 8. This is how the adjustable angle guide first pictured in Fig. 1 is used to saw a 45° angle.

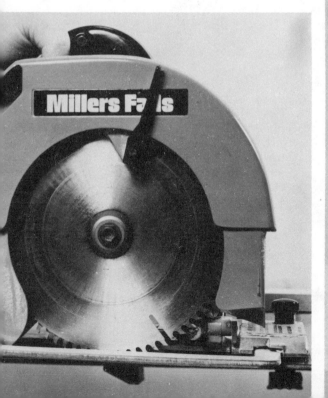

Fig. 9. A jig for making long straight cuts in panelboard when doing interior finish work can be made by supporting the panel to be cut on a piece of 1″ × 6″ or 1″ × 8″ board placed on sawhorses. On top of the panel, mark the location of the cut at one end and place the saw blade at the mark. Make a second mark at the right edge of the saw's sole plate, measure the distance from the left side of the panel to the second mark and mark this distance at the top of the panel. Clamp a perfectly straight length of 1″ × 4″ or 1″ × 6″ lumber with its left edge on both marks and clamp it in place at each end so that the clamps will hold the top board (which is the saw-guide), the panel, and the supporting board. Keeping the saw's sole plate firmly against the top board, make the cut.

Fig. 10. Slide the left side of the saw's sole plate along the top board to make a straight, easy cut. Although for purposes of this picture the portion of the panel being sawed is not supported from below, always use a length of 1″ × 6″ or 1″ × 8″ below the panel 1″ or 2″ to the right of the saw blade.

Fig. 11. A saber saw makes notched cuts and pocket cuts with square inside corners. The round blade of a circular saw leaves a bit of wood in each corner when the blade stops at the cutline: the corner must then be finished with a saber saw or handsaw. And a saber saw can be used when working on a ladder, or in cramped quarters or positions where a circular saw would be clumsy, perhaps impossible, to handle readily.

Fig. 12. Make full use of the many accessories available for electric drills. Hole saws, such as the one illustrated, cut openings for pipes and small ducts; in addition, your electric drill provides power for such other accessories as sanding disks and drums, wire brushes, countersinks, burrs, circular rasps, edgers, and others. It can also be used to drive and remove screws.

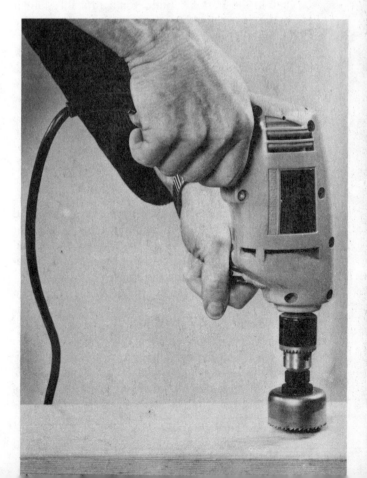

LUMBER

Now let's get down to the materials you'll be using. Going back to our original premise, the assumption is that you're totally unfamiliar with the subject. Whether you are or not, we need at this point to establish frames of reference that will insure complete understanding of the terms used later on. At the same time, you'll need to know how to translate the specifications that appear on plans into the language you'll use in figuring out what you'll need if you modify a plan, or when you place an order with a lumberyard or building supply house. No pretense has been made of trying to provide a complete résumé of the constantly changing field of building materials. The paragraphs below will include only the most frequently used items, and special materials for special applications will be covered in the chapters in which they first appear.

Lumber grading is as good a place as any to begin. First, though, it might be wise to preface any discussion of grade designations with the information that the woods you'll use will be softwoods: white pine, yellow pine, Douglas fir, and, for some special applications, redwood. If you live in the East or South, you'll probably find it better to substitute cypress or cedar where weather resistance and imperviousness to moisture and decay are desired. You might, depending on where you live, find it economical to use *treated lumber* instead of redwood, cedar, or cypress. Treated lumber is impregnated with insect-repelling and moisture-resisting, decay-inhibiting chemicals.

Lumber is designated by two major grades, *select* and *common,* and by subgrades No. 1, No. 2, and No. 3. These grades are applied at the sawmills by inspectors independent of the mills. Their judgments are based on over a hundred different points, including such obvious ones as the number of knots and flaws a board shows and less obvious flaws such as pitch pockets, wormholes, checks or splits and stains.

Unless they feature specialty woods, or happen to be located in a forest-industries area, few lumber dealers today carry an extensive stock of the top grades of lumber. Most No. 1 select and No. 2 select goes under long-term contracts to furniture factories and wood products fabricators, though most dealers will have a limited stock of No. 2 select or No. 1 common, either of which is

suitable for applications such as cabinets and paneling where the wood surface is exposed.

For a majority of framing and concealed applications where normal structural strength is required and perfect appearance is not a factor, No. 2 common lumber is used. For such uses as sheathing and subflooring, there are No. 3 common lower grade boards designated as *form lumber,* though often No. 3 common is used for forms.

Not all lumber is *boards.* This designation applies to lumber less than 2″ thick. Pieces 2″ or more but less than 4″ in thickness are classed as *dimension lumber,* and pieces 4″ or more in thickness are called *timbers.* In yard buildings and similar small structures, timbers will be used very infrequently.

At one time, all lumber was finished to the actual number of inches in width and thickness that are today used in describing boards and dimension lumber. At the turn of the century, a 2″ × 4″ board was actually two full inches thick and four inches wide, a 1″ × 8″ board was a full inch thick and eight inches wide, and so on. Today, these descriptive terms are called *nominal dimensions,* and all boards are actually ¼″ to ½″ thinner and ½″ to ¾″ narrower than the nominal dimensions indicate.

Thus, a 2″ × 4″ is really 1½″ thick and 3½″ wide; a 1″ × 2″ is ¾″ thick and 1½″ wide; a 1″ × 8″ is ¾″ thick and 7½″ wide. You must take these *actual* dimensions into consideration when figuring out how many boards of what length will be required to cover X square feet of surface area. Nominal and actual dimensions are given in a table in Appendix A.

Usually, 2″ lumber is used in a building's *frame.* The framing members, starting from the foundation, are called *sills, floor headers* or *stringers, floor joists, sole plates, studs, top plates, ceiling joists,* and *rafters.* You'll meet these and a few others later, they are described in detail in the next chapter.

Boards used in the *subfloor, sheathing,* and *roof decking* are usually 1″ × 8″, 1″ × 10″ or 1″ × 12″. Today, *plywood, particleboard, hardboard,* or *gypsum board* have largely replaced lumber in sheathing and decking. We'll get better acquainted with these, too, later on, both their place in the building's structure and the materials themselves.

As mentioned earlier, lumber is priced by the

board foot, a measurement of volume rather than area, and prices are based on the nominal dimensions. Though a board described as a 1″ × 12″ is actually only ¾″ thick and 11½″ wide, it is considered to be 1″ × 12″ in pricing. You really don't need to worry greatly about board feet except when figuring coverage. You'll order by nominal dimension plus length, and the dealer will convert your order into board feet when he figures out your bill.

Retail lumber dealers today generally stock boards and dimensional lumber in widths from 2″ to 12″, thicknesses of 1″ and 2″, and lengths from 8′ to 24′ in increments of 2′: 8′, 10′, 12′, and so on. Generally, you'll figure out how many boards of a given width, thickness, and length you'll need and order them as "twenty 1″ × 8″s 24′ long," and the dealer will do the rest.

Dimensional lumber and timbers are usually stocked by retail dealers in thicknesses of 2″, 4″, 6″, 8″, and 10″, in widths from 4″ to 12″, and lengths up to 24′. About the only dimensional lumber you'll require are 2″ × 4″s and 4″ × 4″s with an occasional timber 4″ × 8″ or 4″ × 10″ to make a long header over a garage door, for example.

PANELBOARD

Panelboard is the generic term used to describe all sheet building material sold in 4′ × 8′ panels. There are a number of types of panelboard. The most familiar is *plywood,* made by gluing thin plies of wood together with the grain of each ply at an angle to the next. *Hardboard* panels are made from wood fibers bonded with adhesive material under heat and pressure. *Particleboard* is produced by a similar process using wood chips, sawdust, and other material that was once wasted. Particleboard is often mistakenly called chipboard, which is a type of cardboard. *Gypsum board* is made by sandwiching a core of gypsum between thick sheets of treated paper.

Panelboards are generally sized 4′ × 8′, but you can get them up to 10′ or 12′ on special order. Thicknesses range from ¼″ to ⅞″, and in the case of plywood and particleboard, up to 1½″. The extra-thick panels are used in flooring, and they allow you to install subfloor and finish floor in one operation. (The use of *finish* in flooring means the floor is ready for a carpet or vinyl covering.) All panelboards are available in mois-

ture-resistant exterior grades for use as sheathing and decking. Plywood and hardboards are also available for siding, and these as well as gypsum board come with finished surfaces for use as interior wall paneling.

All panelboards are priced by the square foot, and all sizes are actual, 4′ by 8′, 10′, or 12′. Some lumber dealers will cut panelboards in halves or quarters, but for the most part you'll be expected to buy full sheets.

ROOFING MATERIALS

Roofing or *roof covering* materials are *shingles, shakes, composition shingles,* and *roll roofing.* Shingles are usually made from cedar, though some mills turn out redwood shingles; both woods are available as shakes, an extra-thick type of shingle. Composition shingles are made from asbestos bonded with a tarlike, semirigid medium, and better grades of roll roofing are made from the same material, though there are low-cost roll roofings in which the fibers are paper. The composition roof coverings have a tough, granulated outside coating.

Shingles and shakes are sold in *bundles,* each of which covers 25 square feet when 5″ of the thick end is exposed. Composition shingles are also sold in bundles, sometimes called *squares.* Each bundle covers 100 square feet with a 5″ exposure. Thickness of composition roofings is expressed in terms of weight, the number of pounds that the shingles covering 100 square feet will weigh. The normal standard is 240 pound shingles, written as 240#. Roll roofing thickness is also expressed in the weight of enough material to cover 100 square feet; the standard roll is 50′ long and 3′ wide.

To prevent moisture penetrating through the wooden walls of a house from outdoors, and to assure that roofs are weathertight, an impervious film called a *vapor barrier* is placed between sheathing and siding or studs and siding, and between roof decking and roof covering. This vapor barrier is usually asphalt-treated felt, usually called *felt* but sometimes called *tar paper.* Polyethylene film is widely used as a vapor barrier today. Both materials are sold by the 100′ roll, in varying widths.

MOLDINGS

A variety of decorative moldings in various

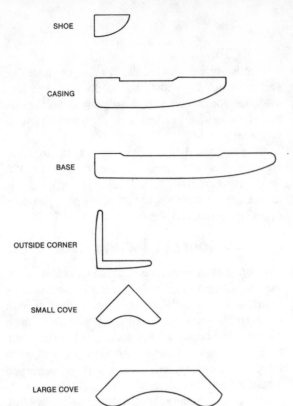

SHOE

CASING

BASE

OUTSIDE CORNER

SMALL COVE

LARGE COVE

Fig. 13. Here are cross sections of some of the most-used interior moldings. Shoe, or base shoe, is used at wall-to-floor or wall-to-ceiling joints. Casing is used as trim on the frames for windows and doors. Base is used at wall-to-floor joints. Outside corner molding is used at corners of gypsum board walls. The two sizes of cove molding are used according to taste at wall-to-ceiling joints.

shapes are used to cover joins (the spaces between wall paneling and floor or ceiling) when finishing interiors. The most common are *cove,* used around the perimeters of room ceilings and *baseboard* and *base shoe,* used along the wall-floor join and installed after the floor covering is laid. A V-shaped and an L-shaped *corner molding* is sometimes applied vertically in panelled rooms. Moldings come in various widths and are priced by the running foot.

NAILS

Nails come in an almost infinite variety of sizes and types, many of the types being for special applications. Flat-headed nails called *common* nails are the kind you'll use most often. *Finishing* nails have small heads with putty-filled countersinks, covered with paint. *Casing* nails, which have conical heads and a slightly larger diameter-to-length ratio than finishing nails, are used when door and window frames are fitted; they, too, are countersunk. *Gypsum board* nails have a rust-resistant coating, oversized heads, and short shanks. *Roofing* nails are very similar to gypsum nails, also coated and short with oversized heads. *Box* nails are thinner than common nails and are used close to the ends of boards and when nailing into end-grain lumber, to avoid splitting.

Nail sizes are expressed in *pennyworths,* abbreviated British style as *"d."* Their sizing is another holdover from the past. It came into use when all nails were handmade in small blacksmith shops; the smiths sold a hundred nails for a certain price, perhaps tenpence for a hundred larger nails or eightpence for a hundred smaller ones. Today, nails are still described as eightpenny or tenpenny written 8d or 10d, and so on. The smaller the number, the smaller the nail.

Pricing of nails is by the pound, and a chart in Appendix B shows nail sizes as well as the average number per pound. You'll use 8d, 12d, and 16d common nails for framing, 6d and 8d finishing nails for installing interior trim, and roofing nails, gypsum board nails, and a few casing nails.

We'll begin to use this building vocabulary in the next chapter when we take a look at the construction and finishing jobs common to all yard buildings. While technical language has been avoided as far as possible, it's the easiest to use in the long run when discussing such specialized subjects as building.

This is especially true in the *bills of materials* at the end of most chapters. The bill of materials simply lists all the items and their quantities that will be needed in a given building. In this book, a departure has been made from normal trade practice; a bill of materials usually lists all items by size without reference to the places they'll be used. In the bills of materials following the chapters, the use of all materials is specified.

It's been done this way because many home craftsmen don't order all their materials at once but buy them as needed or as the budget permits. And, because so many of the building plans you'll look at in later chapters give options in finish and trim as well as size, not all of the materials these jobs call for are included. That's been left up to you, after you've decided what you want. So, check the bills of materials closely, delete items you won't need, and add others that you'll be using.

CHAPTER THREE

Basic Procedures

To save a lot of repetition, all of the basic jobs that you'll run into no matter what type of yard building you decide to put up are covered in this chapter. Those few jobs that are unique to a specific building will be detailed in the appropriate chapter.

Building anything, from a toolshed to a three-story mansion, is simply a matter of cutting boards to a lot of different lengths and fitting them together in a certain sequence. The sequences are for the most part standard. They've been worked out by trial and error over many years, and in many cases by scientific research. Please take it for granted that they represent the best, if not always the easiest, way to go about the job. And be sure you measure accurately and follow the routines given so that everything will come out right.

Do remember to check the bill of materials given at the end of each chapter if you decide to change the size of a building or exercise any of the options that are suggested. Make any necessary changes in the bill of materials so you'll be sure to get only the materials you'll need without forgetting any—especially the optional materials.

Going back to assumptions, as we did in Chapter Two, let's take it for granted that you don't know the first principles of building and that you're depending on this book to provide you with all the information you'll need to carry a yard building job to a successful conclusion, from foundation to finish. This means a lot of details will be covered. If you encounter procedures with which you're already familiar, feel free to skip. Just be sure you *are* familiar with them, though. Now, we'll start at square one.

DIMENSIONS

Dimensions are exceedingly important in building. Common practice today is to build in 4' modules, which means spaces that are multiples of 4 or divisible by 4: 8, 12, 16, 20, etc. Consequently, most building materials are available in these lengths or widths, to reduce waste in cutting.

You'll encounter a few variances from the 4' module on the bills of materials, but you'll also notice that a 10' board is 2½ times a 4' module, which means that what appears to be a 2' long piece of waste lumber will be used somewhere else.

If you change the dimensions of any of the buildings as planned, you'll save yourself a lot of fuss, muss, and bother by staying with the 4' module.

Your building job begins with establishing the exact outline or perimeter of your yard building on the spot you've selected as its location. You will have taken into consideration the relationship of the new building to other structures, house, garage, and so forth, already on your property. Keeping this relationship in mind, you'll have decided on the new building's orientation, which in most cases means squaring it up so that its wall lines will be in harmony with those of other buildings.

LOCATING FOUNDATION LINES

Now the time has come to locate the precise foundation lines. For this job you'll need a hammer, handsaw, tape, framing square, spirit level, and a lot of chalk line. (Old fishing line serves

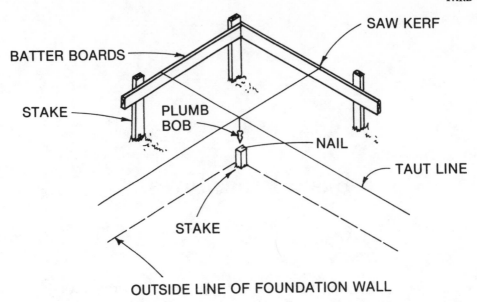

SAW KERF

BATTER BOARDS

STAKE

PLUMB
BOB

NAIL

TAUT LINE

STAKE

OUTSIDE LINE OF FOUNDATION WALL

Fig. 14. **Installation of a set of batter boards is shown here; a similar set is required for each building corner. Placed about 4′ from the actual foundation lines, the batter boards provide a reference point when corner stakes are moved during foundation excavations.**

equally well in this case, for no chalk will be used.) The materials needed are twelve lengths of 2″ × 4″ about 3′ long, with one end of each sharpened to make a stake; four short lengths of 2″ × 2″—about 12″ long; eight 1′ × 4′ or 1′ × 6′ boards about 3′ to 4′ long; and a handful of 8d common nails. And, even though no hard labor is involved, a second pair of hands will save you a lot of time, so if possible enlist a helper.

Drive a 2″ × 2″ stake a few inches into the ground where any corner of your new building will be located. Don't pound it in deeply; it'll probably have to be moved later. Drive a nail in the center of the top of the stake. Measure or pace off the length of one side—any side—of the building and drive a second stake. Repeat this to establish the approximate points where all four corners of the new building will be.

Run a length of chalk line around the four stakes and secure it temporarily. *Measure* each side very exactly. If the two lines marking the ends of the building, or the two lines marking its sides aren't the same length, adjust the stakes as needed and square up each corner as best you can with your framing square. Now step back and study the rectangle outlined by the cord and visualize your new building sitting there. If you de-

cide it should be moved or its orientation changed, now's the time to do it.

When you're satisfied the orientation's the way you want it to be, you must determine the foundation lines with more precision than a framing square will give you. Stretch a length of chalk line diagonally across the rectangle and extend it from one corner for a distance of about 4′. Drive a 2′ × 4′ stake there, squaring up the stake so that one edge and one wide side are parallel with the corner of the rectangle. Do this at all four corners, making sure the stakes are spaced the same distance from the corners.

Drive three other 2″ × 4″ stakes about 3′ from each of the corner 2″ × 2″ stakes, keeping their wide dimensions parallel with an edge and a wide side of the corner stake. Nail two 1′ × 4′ boards (or 1′ × 6′ boards) at right angles to connect the three stakes at each corner. Fig. 14 shows how the finished job should look at each corner. The 1′ × 4′s are called *batter boards*. They will remain in place until the foundation of the new building is finished. The reason for setting them away from the foundation line is to get them located where work on the foundation, digging and so on, won't disturb them. These batter boards are your constant reference points for all

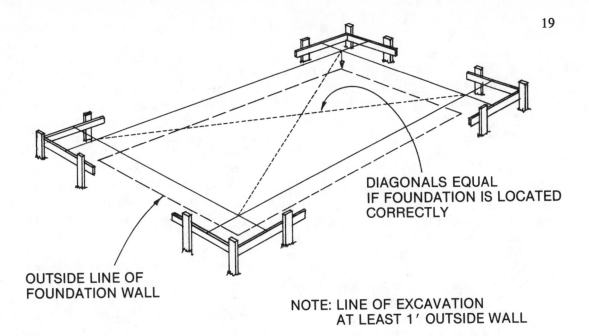

DIAGONALS EQUAL
IF FOUNDATION IS LOCATED
CORRECTLY

OUTSIDE LINE OF
FOUNDATION WALL

NOTE: LINE OF EXCAVATION
AT LEAST 1′ OUTSIDE WALL

Fig. 15. **This is the complete batter board installation. As explained in detail in the text,** **the batter boards are also used to square up the foundation lines.**

horizontal and vertical measurements that have to do with the building's foundation.

Make one batter board by nailing two 1″ × 6″ boards 3′ to 4′ long to a 2″ × 2″ stake at right angles, as illustrated. Nail other 2″ × 2″ stakes to the ends of each board. Drive the stakes into the ground 3′ to 4′ diagonally from one of the corner stakes already set. Level the two boards by placing a spirit level on top of the boards, one end resting on each board, and tap the stakes into the ground until the two boards are leveled in relation to each other.

Make and install batter boards at the other three corners, and use a chalk line and line level to level the batter boards at each corner in relationship to the first. When you have done this, a chalk line stretched around all four batter boards will show that the boards are all on the same horizontal plane, and a framing square will show that each set of batter boards forms a right angle.

Cut a shallow saw kerf in the top edge of each batter board, each cut equally distant from the center of the board's corner stake. The cuts should be 24″ to 30″ from the stake's center.

Now, run a chalk line from kerf to kerf as illustrated (Fig. 15). The four points at which the lines cross should be exactly above the original

2″ × 2″ stakes you drove to mark the foundation line. They probably won't be, of course. Before moving the stakes, check the batter boards' locations by stretching a chalk line diagonally across the foundation between the batter boards. Measure the exact length of the chalk line between the batter boards. Repeat this measurement on the opposite diagonal. When the length of the chalk line between both sets of diagonal corners is precisely the same, your batter boards are aligned.

To get this result, you may have to cut other kerfs in the batter boards, or you may have to move the boards a bit. Be sure to mark over old cuts when a new one is made, or shave a chip off the bottom edge of one of the boards and fill the old saw kerf.

When the four lines stretched from the batter boards form a true rectangle or square directly above the foundation's perimeter, reset the 2″ × 2″ foundation stakes directly below the points at which the chalk lines cross. Use a plumb bob, or tie a heavy nut to the end of a short length of line, to establish a common level for the top of each foundation stake. Tie a knot in the plumb bob line and use it as a reference point in measuring this height. With the knot on the batter board lines, the tip of the plumb bob should just touch the foundation stake.

Later, when you begin digging and leveling, a chalk line from kerf to kerf of your batter boards will allow you to check postholes, trenches, utility entrances, and other key items for accuracy of location and level.

LAYING THE FOUNDATION

About half the buildings for which plans are given in later chapters can be built on a simple post-and-beam foundation. The others will stand on poured concrete foundations because they have slab floors. You can handle the post foundations by yourself quite easily. They require only a few shallow holes and a small amount of concrete. Solid perimeter foundations call for a trench, and when a perimeter foundation and slab floor are used, a substantial amount of concrete will be needed. In addition, the entire floor area must be covered with a layer of sand or small gravel, and reinforcing rods and mesh must be set in place.

You can rent a cement mixer and do the work yourself, of course, but you'll save a lot of time and sweat by having a contractor with power equipment do the digging and leveling. You will also save time by using transit-mixed concrete, which comes to the job in a hopper truck which mixes the concrete en route. My personal experience after having been involved in a number of building projects over a long span of years is that the difference in cost between transit-mixed concrete and that mixed on the job is negligible. Check this for yourself by determining the cost of sand, gravel, water, and sacked cement plus the rental of a mixer, and compare it with the price you're quoted for transit-mix. On any job that calls for more than a couple of yards of concrete, the cost of buying the materials, renting a mixer, and doing the work is likely to differ from the cost of transit-mixed concrete by only a few dollars. In most cases, the cost of hiring a cement contractor for the whole job will be about the same as the materials for the concrete, mixer rental, and the expense of form lumber.

This doesn't apply to post foundations, which are set very quickly and easily. Begin by digging 16″ × 16″ × 16″ holes at each corner of the foundation and extending about 2″ beyond the foundation line. Digging the holes beyond the foundation line means removing the corner

stakes, so you'll use the batter boards to establish the exact size and location of the holes. Spans up to 12′ need only corner posts; for longer spans, set additional posts on centers of about 10′ to 12′. The length of the span will determine the number of additional posts needed.

These holes will be filled with concrete to a common level, determined by measuring down from a batter board line with a plumb bob. If any of the holes is in a low spot or on a slope, make a 16″ × 16″ square form and place it over the hole. Brace the form on each side to hold it in place by nailing short pieces of scrap lumber to the sides of the form, slanting these braces to stakes driven into the ground, and nailing the braces to the stakes, as shown in Fig. 16.

Use No. 3 common or form lumber, 1″ × 6″ or 1″ × 8″, for the forms, framing them with crosspieces on the outsides to form a square. If the forms must be deeper than the width of the lumber used, nail the boards edge to edge after cutting them to the required length. Be sure to oil the insides of the forms with old lubricating oil or whatever kind of oil is available.

Buy ready-to-mix sack concrete to fill the holes to a common level. This material is sold in 80-pound sacks, each sack yielding slightly less than one cubic foot of concrete. You can mix such a small quantity in a wheelbarrow (rented, if you don't own one) or even in an old washtub or garbage pail. The label on the sack gives full instructions, which vary slightly between brands.

Have ready a 16″ to 18″ length of reinforcing bar—called "rebar" by builders—for each side hole and two pieces for each corner hole. These pieces will tie the concrete to the cement blocks on which the building actually rests, and the blocks can't be placed until the concrete of the footings has set. Usually the dealer from whom you buy the rod will lend you a cutter so you can reduce the rod to the lengths you need before you haul it away.

As you fill each hole with concrete, shove a length of the reinforcing rod straight down through the concrete about 6″ from the foundation line and 2″ off-center. Leave 5″ to 6″ of the rod sticking up above the concrete; later, these ends will extend up into the cavities of the cement blocks. If you bend hooks into the ends of the rods, their holding power will be increased. Wait until the concrete is firm before setting the cement blocks. Depending on temperature and

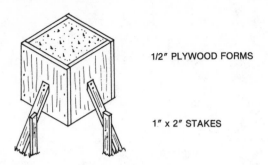

1/2″ PLYWOOD FORMS

1″ x 2″ STAKES

Fig. 16. **Typical forms for pouring a foundation post in post-and-beam floor construction. Be sure the forms are filled to a common level.**

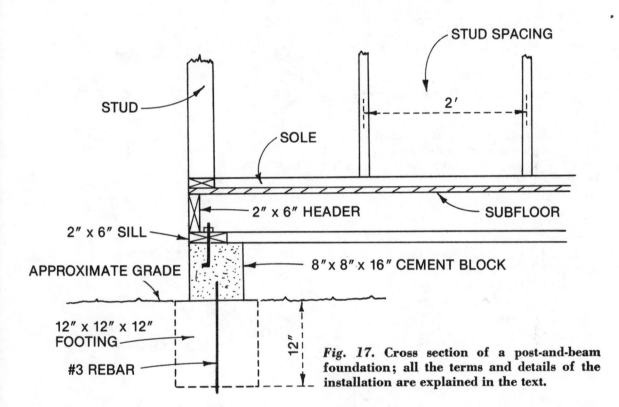

STUD SPACING

2′

STUD

SOLE

2″ x 6″ HEADER

SUBFLOOR

2″ x 6″ SILL

APPROXIMATE GRADE

8″ x 8″ x 16″ CEMENT BLOCK

12″ x 12″ x 12″ FOOTING

12″

#3 REBAR

Fig. 17. **Cross section of a post-and-beam foundation; all the terms and details of the installation are explained in the text.**

humidity, this means forty-five minutes to an hour.

Stretch lines between the batter boards to guide you in setting the blocks. The long sides of the blocks are set parallel to the long sides of the building. Pour concrete into the cavities of the blocks into which rods extend to tie the blocks firmly to the concrete. While the concrete in the block cavities is still soft, push 8″ long anchor bolts into one cavity of each side block and both cavities of each corner block. Leave the nuts on the anchor bolts when you insert them; doing this keeps concrete out of the threads and makes it easier to work with the bolts later.

You've now finished the posts, or piers, of your foundation, and all that's left to do is wait until the concrete cures. To cure thoroughly, allow twenty-four to thirty-six hours. Details of the piers and the framing they support are shown in Fig. 18.

BUILDING ON THE FOUNDATION

You're now ready to set the building's *sills* on the foundation posts. The sills are made from No. 2 common 2″ × 6″ lumber. They form a continuous plate around the bottom of the walls. Sills pieces must be drilled for anchor bolts. The easy way to mark them for drilling is to align the sill pieces with the edges of the cement blocks while resting them on the ends of the anchor

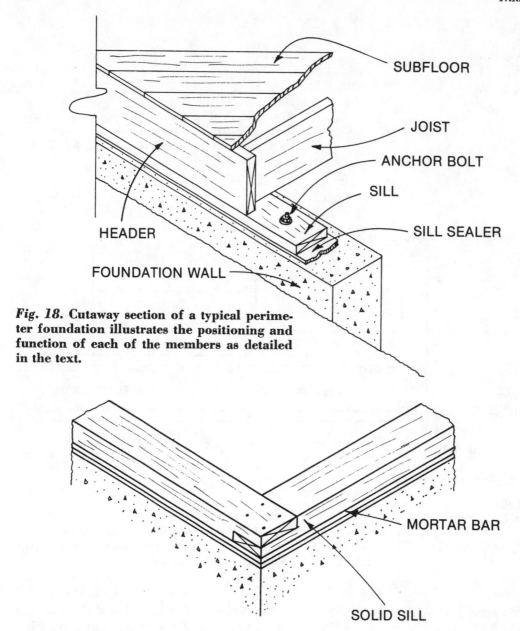

SUBFLOOR

JOIST

ANCHOR BOLT

SILL

SILL SEALER

HEADER

FOUNDATION WALL

MORTAR BAR

SOLID SILL

Fig. 18. **Cutaway section of a typical perimeter foundation illustrates the positioning and function of each of the members as detailed in the text.**

Fig. 19. **This is the approved method of overlapping sill members for maximum strength and rigidity.**

bolts. Tap the lumber with a hammer above each bolt, to leave a dent on the board's underside. Then drill a hole at each dent. Use a drill slightly larger than the diameter of the bolts to give you some leeway in adjusting the sills as you bolt them down.

Check horizontal alignment of the sills with a spirit level. Low spots can be shimmed with strips of cedar shingles to bring them up to level. High spots must be cured by chipping away bits of the supporting pier with a cold chisel.

Now the *foundation header* or *stringer* must be nailed to the sill. This is also made from No. 2 common 2″ × 6″ lumber, set on edge at the outside edge of the sill. The header can be nailed in place after the sill is set, with the nails driven in at an angle—the word for this is "toenailing"—or you can nail header and sill together after the sill is drilled but before it's set on the piers. Run a line of roofing cement between header and sill before nailing them together.

One precaution should be taken. Always let 24″ to 36″ of the header span any joint in the sills. In other words, don't let a sill and a header joint occur at the same place. Stagger them. Another precaution you can take is to nail a short length of 2″ × 4″ or 2″ × 6″ lumber over the joints in both sill and header. Nail this inside the foundation line so the outer side of the header will be neatly finished and smooth.

Next come the *floor joists,* the boards on which the floor will be laid. In a small building these are made from No. 2 common 2″ × 4″ lumber set across the building's narrow dimension. However, if the span is greater than 10′ to 12′, use No. 2 common 2″ × 6″ lumber. Set the joists on 24″ centers. This measurement is abbreviated as *24″ OC,* and simply means that the center of the edge of each joist is spaced 24″ from the joists on either side of it.

Nail through the header into the butts of the joists with 16d common nails and toenail with 12d nails into the corners where joist and header meet. If you use 2″ × 6″ lumber for the joists, the ends will have to be notched so their upper edges will be level with the top of the header. Set cross-joists on 24″ centers between the long joists. Cross-joists are needed to give a properly spaced nailing surface for the floorboards, as well as to brace the main joists when these cover long spans.

Next comes the floor. You have several options here. A *subfloor* of No. 3 common 1″ × 8″, 1″ × 10″, or 1″ × 12″ boards or shiplap, which has overlapping edge joints, can be nailed to the floor joists. You can also use 4″ × 8″ plywood or particleboard panels, ¾″ thick. Another option is to use special 4′ × 8′ panels of plywood and particleboard which combine subfloor and finish floor and on which the final covering, carpet or plastic tile, can be laid.

If a board floor is used, the board should be nailed diagonally at a 45° angle to the joists. If 4′ × 8′ panels are used, they should be laid so that there is no point at which four corners come

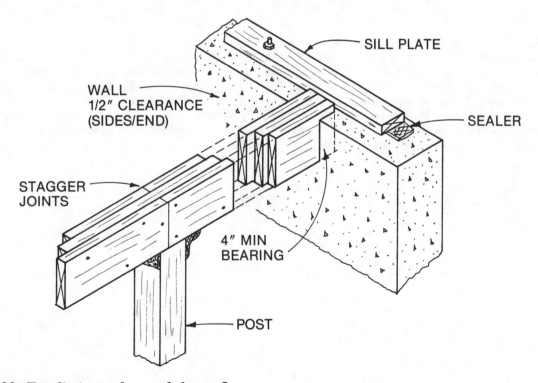

Fig. 20. **To eliminate the need for a floor header, floor joists are often dropped into pockets in the concrete perimeter footings as shown here.**

Fig. 21. This detail of floor joists shows the cross-joists that are required for installation of a plywood or fiberboard subfloor. Much less elaborate cross bracing is required for subfloors of diagonally nailed boards. For panelboards, the floor joists are spaced 24″ OC, with cross-joists also spaced 24″ OC to provide nailing surfaces for the panels.

Fig. 22. To lay a subfloor using 4′ × 8′ panelboards, begin with a half sheet as shown here. This eliminates the potential trouble spot which could be caused by having four corners of the panelboards come together. The first piece nailed in place is the half sheet, upper left; the remaining half sheet is the last piece nailed in place at the corner diagonally opposite.

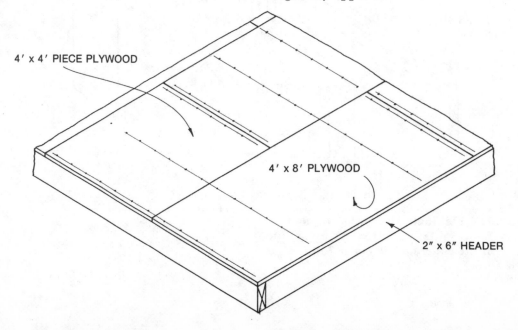

4′ x 4′ PIECE PLYWOOD

4′ x 8′ PLYWOOD

2″ x 6″ HEADER

Fig. 23. This studding, assembled on the concrete slab, is in the process of being erected. Note the headers and cripple studs in the right-hand side wall, designed for a large fixed-sash window.

together. Saw one panel in half and install it in a corner first to avoid a four-corner-meeting joint, using the other half on the final course. Fig. 22 shows how this is done.

With the flooring nailed in place, assemble the wall *studding*. This is made from No. 2 common 2″ × 4″s. The studding assembly has four components (See Fig. 23). The *sole* or *sole plate* goes next to the flooring around the building's perimeter. To the soles, the studs are nailed at right angles to rise vertically. The *first* or *lower top plate* is nailed to the top of the studs and the section of studding is erected and nailed in place. Put on the *upper top plate* after the section is erected, with the ends overlapping the joints of the lower top plate at each corner. An 8′ or 10′ section of studding is about all one person can

handle, but with a helper you can assemble an entire wall for erection.

To build studding, use the floor as a work area and assemble it flat. Studs for a room with an 8′ ceiling will be the height of the inside wall minus three inches, the width of the sole and lower top plates. Thus, the studs are 7′9″ long. Nail through the sole plate into the ends of the studs with 16d common nails, setting the studs on 16″ centers if board sheathing is used, 24″ OC if the exterior will be covered with panelboard. Finally, nail through the first top plate into the top ends of the studs after being sure the assembly is squared up with a framing square.

If you use two or more lengths of lumber for plates, nail through the ends of the sole plate into the floor at joints. If two or more lengths of lumber are used for top plates, be sure the joints in the bottom plate are overlapped by solid lumber on the upper plate and nail the ends of the lower plate to the upper at each joint. A gusset of ½″ thick plywood can be added across joints to reinforce them if you wish.

When the studding is assembled, raise it on the

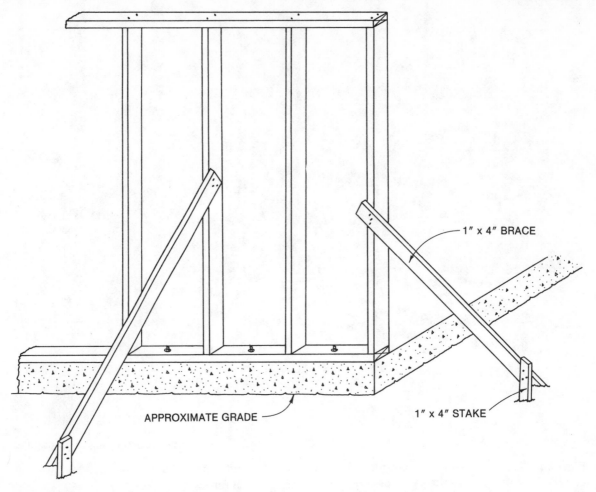

1" x 4" BRACE

APPROXIMATE GRADE

1" x 4" STAKE

Fig. 24. **Brace studding assemblies after they are aligned by tack-nailing diagonal braces to stakes driven 3′ to 4′ from the foundation line. Braces are removed after all the studding has been installed and tied together.**

sole plate and slide it into position. Don't worry at this point about aligning it vertically, you'll do that a bit later. Nail between the studs into the floor with 16d common nails. The outside edge of the sole plate must be flush with the side of the floor header along each wall.

Align the stud assembly vertically with a spirit level and hold it in place with braces of 1″ × 4″ lumber nailed diagonally from studding to the floor at each corner and in the center. (See Fig. 24.) Next, assemble the studding for a wall that joins the studding now in place and erect, align, and brace it. Tie the two assemblies together where they meet by toenailing 10d or 12d common nails into the corner studs. Then assemble,

raise, align, and set the remaining two assemblies just as you did the first two.

Now, put on the upper top plate, nailing it to the lower top plate. Remember to overlap corner joints with the upper plate.

WINDOWS AND DOORS

Window and door openings are framed with *headers,* which are horizontal members nailed between the studs on each side of the studs removed to make the opening, and by *trimmer studs,* which are nailed vertically between the plates and the top and bottom headers (Fig. 26). The placement of the trimmer studs establishes the width of the window or door openings; both the headers and trimmer studs are spaced to allow a bit of extra room on all sides of the window or doorframe. The frames are trued up between the headers and trimmer studs by wedges made from shingles or scrap lumber. The purpose of the headers and trimmers is to distribute the

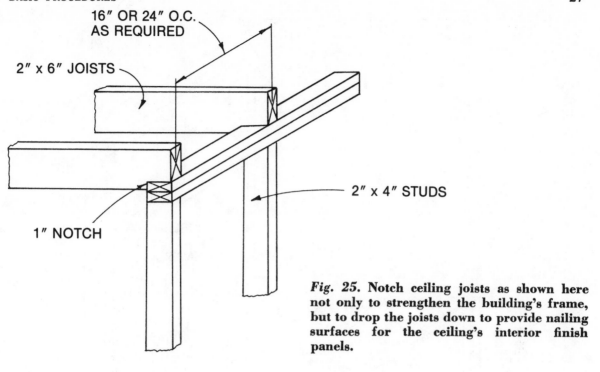

16" OR 24" O.C.
AS REQUIRED

2" x 6" JOISTS

2" x 4" STUDS

1" NOTCH

Fig. 25. **Notch ceiling joists as shown here not only to strengthen the building's frame, but to drop the joists down to provide nailing surfaces for the ceiling's interior finish panels.**

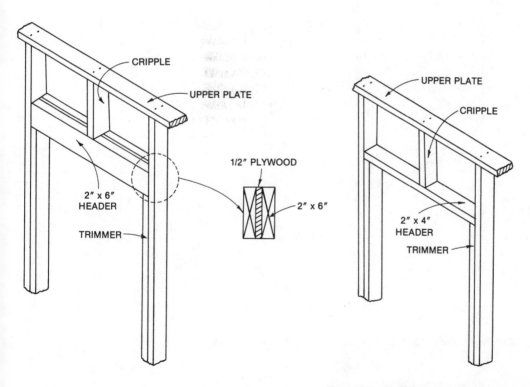

CRIPPLE

UPPER PLATE

1/2" PLYWOOD

2" x 6"

2" x 6"
HEADER

TRIMMER

UPPER PLATE

CRIPPLE

2" x 4"
HEADER

TRIMMER

Fig. 26. **Follow the details of this drawing and the step-by-step instructions in the text to frame door openings.**

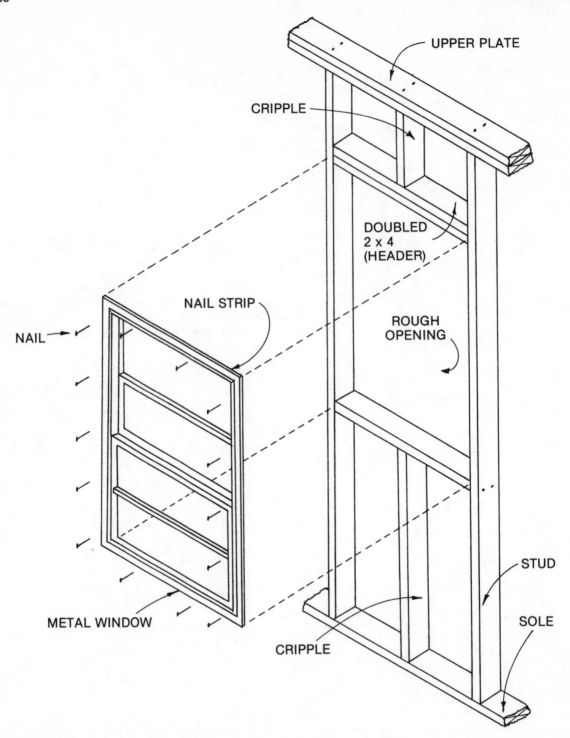

Fig. 27. This sketch provides details for framing window openings.

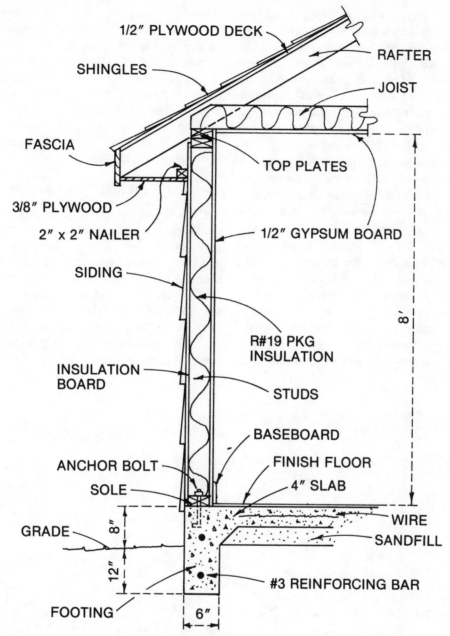

Fig. 28. A cross section of a typical wall assembly, including optional insulation.

load placed by the roof on the wall's top plates onto the studs on either side of the door or window.

Headers in *load-bearing* walls, which include all four outside walls and some inside partition walls, need to be stronger and more rigid than those placed in *non-load-bearing* walls. In load-bearing walls, make the headers of doubled 2″ × 6″s installed on edge, with a spacer of ½″ plywood between them to make the headers the same width as the studs they join. In non-load-bearing walls the headers can be made from doubled 2″ × 4″s nailed flat. Door openings require only top headers, window openings require headers at both the top and bottom of the frame. The bottom headers in windows 4′ wide or less can be a single 2″ × 4″; in wider spans use doubled 2″ × 4″s.

When measuring for headers, begin at the bottom of one of the studs that will be cut to make the window opening; measure from the sole plate to the point where the bottom of the window frame is desired. Mark this point, and measure from it to the point where the top of the frame will come. Mark it. Subtract from the bottom mark the width of the header plus ½″ to ¾″ and mark the cutline. Do the same thing at the top frame line. If more than one stud is to be removed, mark the others with the cutline you've established. Saw out the section of stud or studs.

Measure the distance between the uncut studs on each side of the opening and cut the headers this length. Nail through the studs into the ends of the headers with 16d common nails and then toenail with 10d nails at each header-stud joint. This includes the studs which have been cut to make the opening.

Cut the trimmer studs from the sections removed to accommodate the headers and toenail them at the proper width between the headers to frame the window casing. Remember to allow ½″ to ¾″ on each side so the casing or frame can be shimmed in place. Door headers are installed only at the top of the opening, and the sole plate is then sawed off flush with the inner sides of the trimmer studs and the sawed-out section is removed. Short studs called *cripples* are nailed to the top plate and headers. These should be spaced 12″ to 14″ OC from the original studs between plate and header.

CEILINGS AND ROOFS

Ceiling joists go into place next. These are made from No. 2 common 2″ × 4″s for short spans 10′ or less, 2″ × 6″ for spans longer than 10′. These joists are spaced 24″ OC, with measurement beginning from one end of the building. If when the other end of the building is reached, say 28″ or 30″ remain to be spanned, install a joist 24″ from the last joist rather than splitting the difference. Otherwise you'll encounter problems when putting up the ceiling.

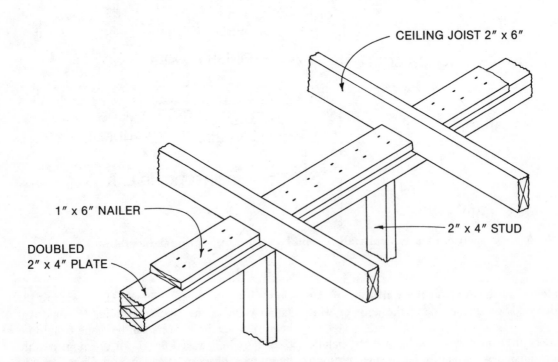

Fig. 29. **If the interior of a building is to be finished with a panelboard ceiling, boards must be placed between the ceiling joists as shown to provide nailing surfaces for the ceiling panels.**

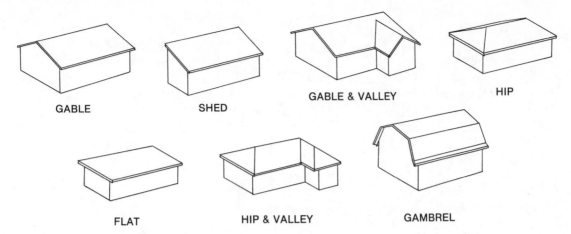

GABLE   SHED   GABLE & VALLEY   HIP

FLAT   HIP & VALLEY   GAMBREL

Fig. 30. Here are the types of roofs commonly used, not only on yard buildings, but also on dwellings. You may want to vary some of the plans given in the book to have the roof of your yard building match that of your home.

Cross-joists are placed on 48″ centers between the long main ceiling joists. These not only brace the main joists but provide nailing surfaces for the panelboard ceiling. Provide nailing surfaces along the top plates by nailing lengths of 1″ × 2″ cut from scrap boards between the joists, the bottom edges of these pieces flush with the bottom edge of the upper top plate.

Next come the *rafters,* and these will vary according to the type of roof the building will have. There are two basic types of roofs: *flat* and *gable.* All other roof lines are a variation of these two. Flat roofs are aligned horizontally with the building's foundation line. When a flat roof is given a slant for better drainage, it is then called a *shed* roof, and the angle of the slant is called the *pitch.* *Gable* roofs rise unbroken to a peak; if the gable is given pitched ends it becomes a *hip* roof. Other variations are shown in Fig. 30. The point is that each type of roof requires a different kind of framing in the rafters.

When a flat roof is being built, the rafters are simply nailed on 24″ centers across the top plates; they should span the narrow dimension of the building. An overhang, or *eave,* is created by extending them beyond the building wall. When the extension is carried beyond the ends of the building, a separate rafter assembly must be used; these are called *lookout* rafters (Fig. 32). Depending on the span involved, rafters can be made from No. 2 common 2″ × 4″s or 2″ ×

6″s. If a shed roof is being installed, its pitch can be obtained either by raising the front wall or lowering the rear wall.

Gable roofs rise from the top plates to a peak above the building's center. The rafters are joined at the peak by a board running at a right angle to them, the *ridgeboard.* All types of gabled roofs, regardless of style, use a ridgeboard (Fig. 33).

A roof's pitch is determined by the angle at which it rises. Pitch is expressed in terms of inches of roof to inches of rise, and is written or abbreviated in figures; thus, a 12/6 pitch is a rise of 6″ to each 12″, a 12/4 pitch is a rise of 4″ per 12″ and so on.

Gable roofs are frequently supported by *trusses,* which are fabricated on the ground. A truss may be made from No. 2 common 2″ × 4″s; in very wide spans, 2″ × 6″s might be used. However, trusses get their rigidity and strength largely because their joints are reinforced with glued and nailed plywood plates called *gussets.* Fig. 34 shows a typical truss.

Decking, which provides a nailing surface for the roof covering, is nailed over the rafters. The decking may be boards, but today exterior grade panelboard is most commonly used. When applying decking, follow the pattern given to avoid four-corner joints in panel floors (see Fig. 22).

A layer of *felt* (tar paper) or polyethylene film is applied over the decking and provides a vapor barrier. The final roof covering, shingles, shakes,

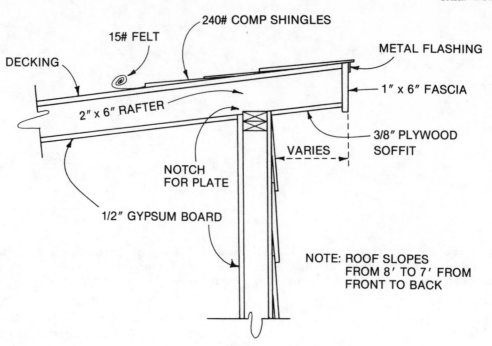

Fig. 31. A cross section of a shed roof. More construction details are given in the text.

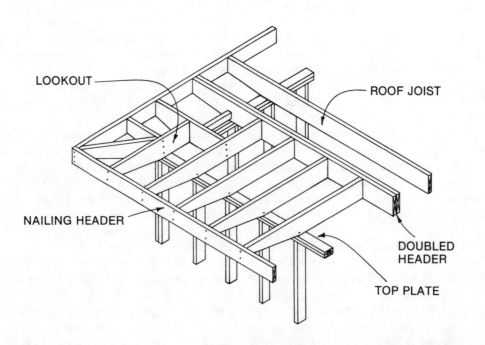

Fig. 32. To extend the roof line of a shed roof from the ends of a building, install the lookout rafters illustrated here.

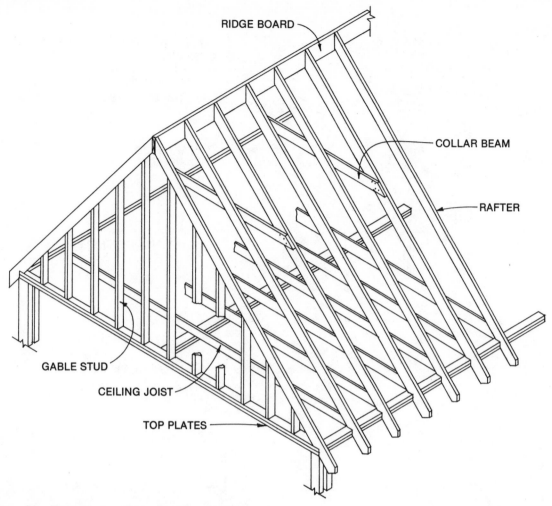

RIDGE BOARD

COLLAR BEAM

RAFTER

GABLE STUD

CEILING JOIST

TOP PLATES

Fig. 33. **Details in this sketch give you a bird's-eye view of the framing members that go into a gabled roof.**

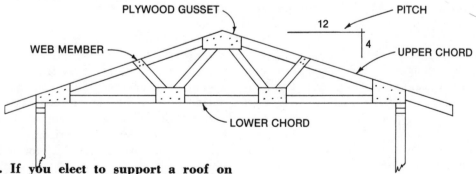

PLYWOOD GUSSET

PITCH

12

4

WEB MEMBER

UPPER CHORD

LOWER CHORD

Fig. 34. **If you elect to support a roof on trusses rather than rafters, the trusses can be fabricated on the ground by following this drawing, and then raised to rest on the top plates. Many weekend builders find this a good alternative, as one man can easily assemble the trusses, and hire help only when setting them.**

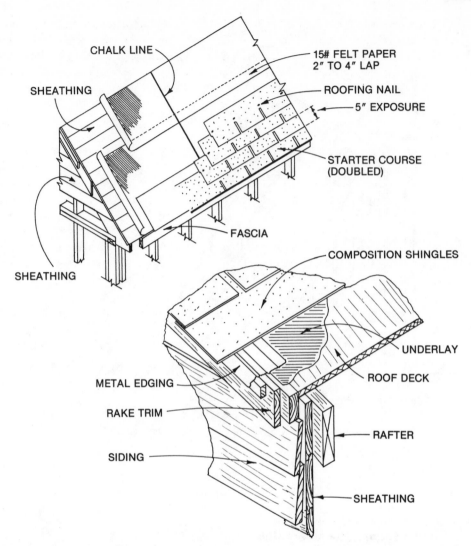

Fig. 35. Cutaways show the details of installing roof coverings. If panelboards are used as decking, refer to Fig. 22; follow the pattern it gives to eliminate the weak spot caused by having four panel corners fall at the same place.

or composition shingles, is then put on. The construction of a typical roof is illustrated in Fig. 35.

OUTSIDE WALLS

Outside wall construction has changed since the introduction of exterior-grade panelboards. Before these appeared, studs in wood frame buildings were set on 16″ centers and *sheathing* of No. 3 common boards was nailed to the studs in diagonal courses, with a finish covering of milled boards, *siding,* then being applied over the sheathing. The great rigidity of panelboards now makes it possible to eliminate sheathing in small buildings in many cases, and to set studs on 24″ centers. Interior bracing between studs has also been virtually eliminated, except when the panelboards are to be installed horizontally, in which case a nailing surface must be provided on 48″ centers.

Sheathing can be considered optional in most of the yard buildings for which this book provides plans. By all means, though, install a vapor barrier between the studs and siding. And, if you live in an area where extremely high winds can be expected, you should consider including sheathing as well as double-nailing the roof deck-ing, sheathing, and siding. Double-nailing simply means spacing nails on 4″ centers instead of the more usual 6″ centers. You will also, if you live in an area of heavy snows, want to increase any roof pitch in the plans. In some sections, pitches of 12/8 or 12/10 are required.

Back now to the subject of siding. You have many options in selecting siding other than those given in the building plans that follow. Because lap siding is perhaps the most traditional of all sidings, it is suggested in a number of the plans; hardboard lap siding is also inexpensive. How-ever, exterior-grade plywood siding in ¾″ and ⅞″ thicknesses goes up faster than lap siding and is somewhat easier to apply. There are many patterns available, and this siding can be applied both vertically and horizontally. A number of patterns can also be had in tempered hardboard sidings.

Should you apply any strip siding, such as lap or shiplap, a course of sheathing should be in-stalled. In this connection, a relatively new gyp-sum board sheathing deserves your attention. Panelboards of this type are treated for weather resistance and have one side covered with alumi-num foil, which serves as a vapor barrier.

FINISHING

Closing the window and door openings is the final step in the construction of your yard build-ing, except for interior finish, which we'll get to in a moment. *Casing* lumber, milled to special di-mensions, is used to frame these openings, but I recommend that rather than spend hours on this difficult job, you should use preframed windows and doors. These units cost very little more than you'd spend on a door or window and the neces-sary casing materials and the hardware required for installation. Preframed units are complete and their installation simple. Because the instal-lation job will vary slightly between units from

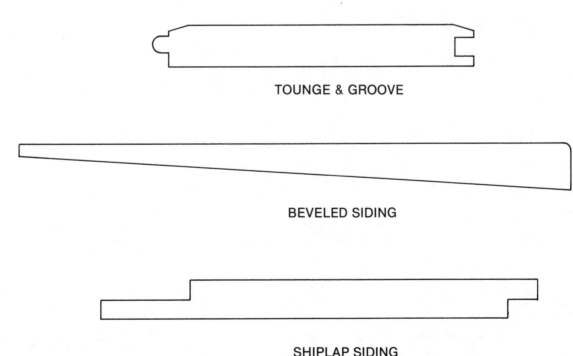

TOUNGE & GROOVE

BEVELED SIDING

SHIPLAP SIDING

Fig. 36. **Shown in profile are the three most common types of board siding. See the text and Appendix A for the method used in figuring wall coverage.**

different manufacturers, no installation details are included here.

Since no two of the yard buildings for which plans are given later have quite the same interior finish, details for this will be given in the individual chapters. So will details for such items as utility entrances and cabinets.

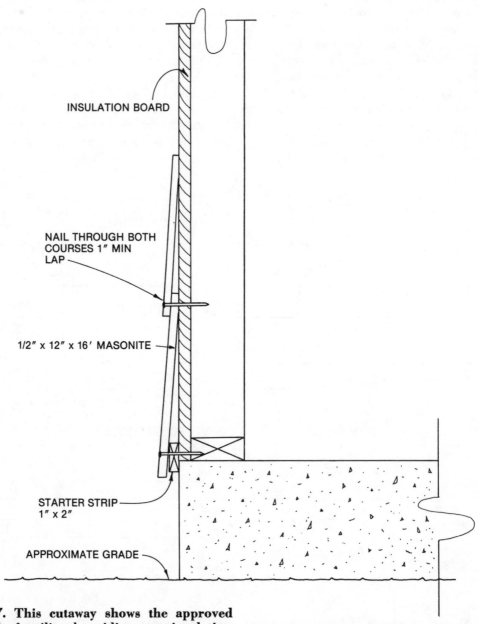

INSULATION BOARD

NAIL THROUGH BOTH COURSES 1″ MIN LAP

1/2″ x 12″ x 16′ MASONITE

STARTER STRIP 1″ x 2″

APPROXIMATE GRADE

Fig. 37. **This cutaway shows the approved method of nailing lap siding over insulation board sheathing.**

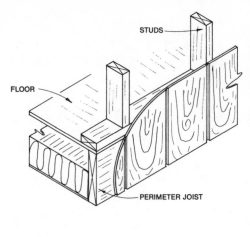

STUDS

FLOOR

PERIMETER JOIST

Fig. 38. Remember that all strip siding, whether lumber or hardboard, must be applied over sheathing, while as this sketch shows, panelboard siding can be installed directly on the studs. However, see the text for details of this installation, including the need for a vapor barrier between the siding and studs.

Fig. 39. Many yard buildings are finished with board and batten siding rather than the more costly formed sidings. This cutaway shows the pattern to follow if you wish to substitute board and batten siding for one of the sidings suggested in the book's plans.

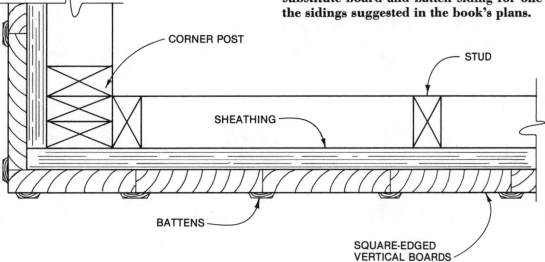

CORNER POST

STUD

SHEATHING

BATTENS

SQUARE-EDGED VERTICAL BOARDS

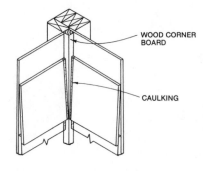

WOOD CORNER BOARD

CAULKING

Fig. 40. Regardless of the type of siding you choose to install on your yard building, this drawing shows how to finish the inside corners to make them weatherproof.

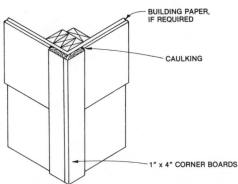

BUILDING PAPER, IF REQUIRED

CAULKING

1″ x 4″ CORNER BOARDS

Fig. 41. This sketch gives corner finishing details for outside corners of buildings covered with any type of sheathing, whether lumber or panelboard.

CHAPTER FOUR

Toolshed

PLANS

What we have here is the simplest of all yard buildings, a small walk-in toolshed for the storage of yard and garden equipment, tools, bikes, and seldom-used household items. It is a barebones building with virtually no frills. Depending on your skill and experience, the shed should require only thirty to thirty-five hours of construction time. Depending on your needs and wishes, it can be used with an unfinished, partly finished, or completely finished interior.

In spite of its simplicity, the building will give you almost 200 square feet of usable floor space under a shed roof that provides for a 7′ ceiling height at the rear and a full 8′ ceiling in the front. The single opening called for in the plan is a door, but at your option you can add a window. However, if you live in an isolated area or one in which pilferage is a problem, limiting access to a door is a way to discourage the casual thief who might be prowling around.

For economy as well as simplicity and ease of construction, the building is planned on a 4′ module, which means that you can use 8′ lumber and 4′ × 8′ sheet materials in erecting it. Simplicity and economy begin with the structure's post-and-beam foundation, and continue through its shed roof, the simplest practical roof with which to cover a small building. If you wish, the plan given can be expanded to give extra space. Should you do this, think in terms of 4′ increments to keep the construction in the easy-to-use, economical 4′ module.

FIRST STEPS

Begin by choosing a site and laying floor level and foundation lines. Follow the procedures detailed in Chapter Three, setting corner stakes and batter boards after doing any necessary leveling of the site. Once this has been done, dig four holes, 12″ × 12″ × 12″, one at each of the corners you've established. The digging will remove the corner stakes, so the usefulness of the batter boards described in Chapter Three becomes obvious. Use the batter boards and a cord to keep the holes dug for the intermediate piers in line. You'll need two holes on 4′ centers for the piers on the building's 16′ dimension, one on a 6′ center on each 12′ side.

From this point on, it's a matter of following the basic procedures detailed in Chapter Three to pour concrete for the foundation piers, put the cement blocks on the piers, and lay the sills and foundation headers on them, attaching these as described. The floor joists and flooring are also installed by the methods given in Chapter Three.

WALL STUDS

Your first variation from the basic construction techniques detailed earlier comes when you begin to cut studs for the walls. In the toolshed you're building, the front wall is 8′ high, the back wall only 7′ high. This is done to give the shed roof the proper pitch. Studs for the front wall, then, will be 7′10″ long, those for the back wall, 6′10″. The studs for the side walls will differ slightly in length, as these walls must slant from front to back as will the roof line.

About the easiest way to cut the side wall studs is to first cut the front and back ones, which are the same length as those used in the front and

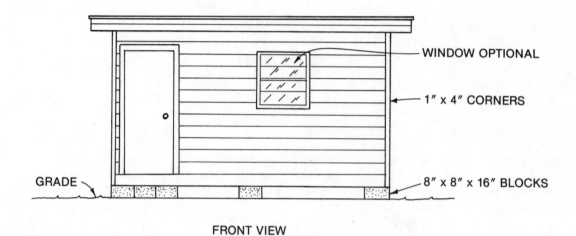

WINDOW OPTIONAL

1″ x 4″ CORNERS

GRADE

8″ x 8″ x 16″ BLOCKS

FRONT VIEW

Fig. 42. Toolshed, front view and floor plan.
Notation above door in floor plan represents
width and height measurements, i.e. door is
3′ wide by 6′8″ high.

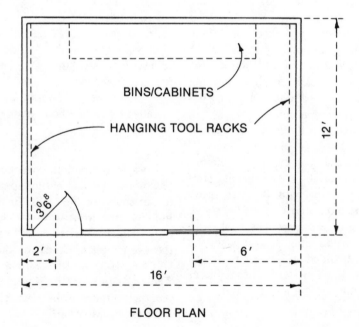

BINS/CABINETS

HANGING TOOL RACKS

12′

$3^{0}6^{8}$

2′

6′

16′

FLOOR PLAN

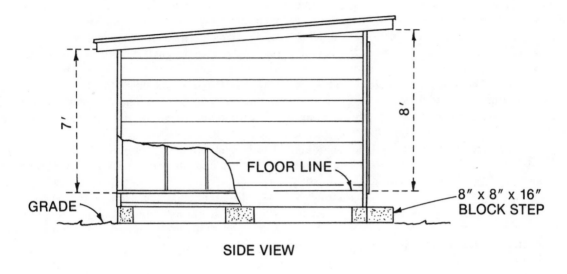

Fig. 43. **Toolshed, side view.**

back walls, and nail the sole plate and lower top plate to these studs. Then with the frame of your stud assembly lying flat, locate and mark the center of the rest of the studs and measure from the inside edge of the sole to the inside edge of the top plate at each centerpoint. Cut each stud according to these measurements, and use them as patterns to mark the studs in the second side wall.

Remember too when planning your studding, that the studs should be on 16″ centers if you're using board sheathing, on 24″ centers if you're using panelboard sheathing. Then proceed according to the methods given in Chapter Three to set headers for the door opening.

RAFTERS

With the headers in place, the studding that will support the walls is also ready to take on the load of the roof. Move on to putting up the rafters. Because the building has a shed roof, the rafter installation is very simple. Ceiling joists are not required, as the rafters will support any ceiling of panelboards that you want to add. You'll only need to put 1′ × 4′ boards on 24″ centers between the rafters to provide nailing surfaces for the ceiling installation.

Use No. 2 common 2″ × 6″ lumber for the rafters. They can be cut from 16′ lengths; the actual rafters will be 14′8″ long, to allow for a 16″

roof overhang at front and back. If you want to add a side overhang as well, see the details given in Chapter Three for the fitting of lookout rafters along the sides.

Notch the rafters at each end where they will rest on the top plates. A saber saw or handsaw can be used to cut the notches, which will be sawed at an angle that produces a snug fit of the rafters against the plates. To save a lot of figuring in establishing the angles at which these notches must be cut, place a 2″ × 6″ across the narrow dimension of the building, resting it on the sole plates between the studs of the front and back walls, and center it on the plates.

Cut a piece of scrap 2″ × 4″ exactly 12″ long; both ends must be square. Lift the end of the 2″ × 6″ that protrudes from the front studding and put the 12″ block under it. Toenail a nail through the 2″ × 6″ into the block. Use the stud against which the rafter is resting as a straight-edge and draw a line across the 2″ × 6″ along the line of the stud. Mark the bottom front edge of the stud at the point where it crosses the outside edge of the stud. Repeat this marking on the other end of the stud where it sticks out beyond the wall of the building.

Lay a framing square with its short side on the mark made at the inside of the plates. Move the corner of the square up with the outside inch markings in line with this mark, measuring toward the center of the rafter, 1″ per foot of pitch. Keeping the short arm of the square on the mark at the edge of the rafter, swing the long arm of the square up to meet the second mark. Draw lines along both arms to the rafter edges. Repeat this at the marks made on the rafter at the plates of the back wall.

Saw out the triangles marked on the rafter edge. The notches created are called *bird's-mouths,* and the short side of the bird's-mouths is parallel to the line at which the rafter must be sawed to align its ends vertically with the building's walls.

Extend a line on the short side of this angle across the face of the rafter, using the framing square as a straightedge. Measure the long side of the bird's-mouth, add 16″ (or any amount of overhang desired) and measure this length from the line on the top and bottom edges of the rafter. The mark at the top of the rafter will extend further than the bottom mark. Connect the

edge marks with a line across the rafter's face; this will be your saw line. Do this at each end of the rafter, saw off excess material, and use the first rafter as a pattern to mark the others for cutting.

Toenail the rafters on 24″ centers to the top plate. Cut spacers to go between the rafters to fill the gaps between the plates and the roof decking, then apply the roof decking on top of the rafters, as already described in Chapter Three. After the decking job is finished, nail on the outside wall sheathing and the siding, again referring to Chapter Three for details. Finally, put on the roofing material. An optional last step in finishing the exterior is the addition of fascia plates over the ends of the rafters and soffits under them. The fascias are made from No. 2 common 1″ × 6″ lumber and the soffit strips can be hardboard or exterior-grade plywood. There are two advantages to completing the exterior this way. First, you make it more weatherproof and second, the fascia and soffits are a lot easier to paint than the protruding rafter ends.

FINISHING

Now we've come to the interior finish of your new toolshed. You can leave it as it is if you wish, with hanging storage for such garden needs as rakes, hoes, and hoses provided simply by nailing 1″ × 2″ or 1″ × 4″ slats across the studs, or protruding from them, at the required height. Hang hoses, etc., on protruding slats, use the slats spanning the open areas between studs for hoes, rakes and so on. Or you can install heavy-duty pegboard, which allows you to use the many pegboard-mounted hangers now available. For shelf storage, bins and cabinets can be built to your taste across the back wall. If dust is a problem, you can get virtually dust-free storage without building cabinet doors. Simply hang widths of tarpaulin-grade plastic sheeting to the top of the shelves. Weight the bottom edges of the sheeting with lengths of lath to hold it taut.

If you intend to store anything that might be damaged by heat or cold, though, you should consider finishing the interior by placing rock wool insulation batts between the rafters and adding interior walls of gypsum board.

Fig. 44. The first step in determining the angles at which to cut rafter notches for shed or gabled roofs is to rest a rafter on edge on the top plate of the stud assembly and with a piece of scrap 2″ × 4″ nestled against the rafter, mark the rafter at each edge of the 2″ × 4″. Be sure the bottom end of the 2″ × 4″ has been sawed square.

Fig. 45. **Place a framing square as shown,
with the square's short arm on the inside
mark and the long arm on the outside mark.
The inch markings on the short arm of the
square are used to determine the roof pitch;
in the picture, a roof pitch of 1″ per foot is
being marked. Draw lines on the rafter along
both arms of the framing square.**

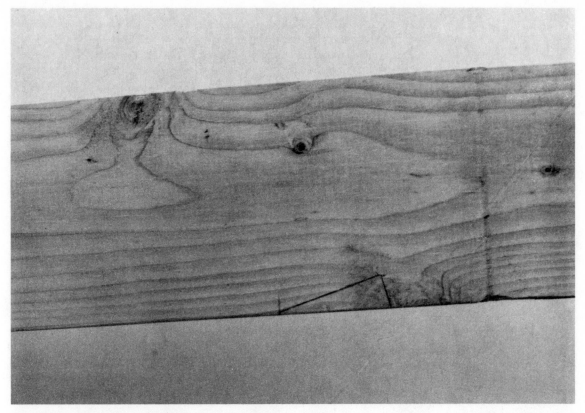

Fig. 46. In the photo, the lines on the rafter mark the triangle that must be cut out with a saber saw or handsaw to produce the roof pitch.

Fig. 47. To determine the angle at which the ends of the rafters must be sawed off to be in vertical alignment with the building's walls, use the framing square to extend the short notch cut, as shown here, after the angle has been marked. Then, transfer this angle to the saw line at the rafter's end as explained in the text.

BILL OF MATERIALS:

Foundation:

- 12 80 pound sacks ready-to-mix concrete
- 9 8″ × 8″ × 12″ cement blocks
- 1 20′ reinforcing bar
- 11 6″ anchor bolts

Framing:

- 5 2″ × 6″ 12′ (sills, floor headers, door and window headers)
- 4 2″ × 6″ 16′ (sills, floor headers, door and window headers)
- 65 2″ × 4″ 8′ (sole and top plates, studding, stud bracing)
- 8 2″ × 4″ 12′ (floor joists)
- 8 2″ × 4″ 20′ (rafters)
- 3 1″ × 6″ 12′ (spacers between rafters)

Exterior:

- 6 4′ × 8′ sheets ¾″ exterior-grade plywood (roof deck)
- 17 1″ × 12″ 16′ lumber or hardboard beveled siding (siding)
- 17 1″ × 12″ 12′ lumber or hardboard beveled siding (siding)
  Or use instead:
- 14 4′ × 8′ sheets ¾″ plywood decorative siding
- 1 100′ roll tar paper (vapor barriers, roof, and exterior walls)
- 2 bundles 240# composition shingles (roofing)

Trim and finish:

- 4 1″ × 4″ 16′ (corner battens)
- 1 2′ × 6′6″ prehung door
- 1 24″ × 36″ prehung window (optional)

Nails:

- 8 pounds 8d common
- 5 pounds 16d common
- 2 pounds roofing

CHAPTER FIVE

Storage/Guesthouse

PLANS

This building as planned has a dual purpose. It can be used either as a general storage building for a large family or, with easy modifications, as a guesthouse. It could also serve as a small efficiency apartment-type rental unit.

In its function as a storage building, it is planned to provide closed storage for out-of-season wardrobes or household items used seasonally or on special occasions, as well as for garden gear, outdoor sports equipment, and so on. Or a small portion of the building could be used for storage and the larger area used as a guest room. With long range preplanning when the building is constructed, these several functions can be accommodated with a minimum of expense and work.

Depending on the amount of interior finishing required for the building in its initial mode, construction time is estimated as fifty to sixty-five hours. The former figure would apply to erecting the building with a minimum of interior finishing, the latter to a complete finishing of the larger of the two inside areas it provides.

As the floor plan shows (Fig. 49), the 24' × 16' building is divided into two sections by a wall. The small section provides 128 square feet of floor space, the larger section 256 feet, for a total interior area of 384 square feet. Some additional storage space can be gained by providing access to its attic. If the building is to be converted into a dwelling, or if the larger section of the building is to be used as guest quarters, a cabinet-type water heater can be installed in the attic space, and a wall-type heater can be set into the partition wall.

In addition, a shower, lavatory, and toilet can be placed in the alcove on the right of the plan. Alternatively, if the building should see later use as a rental unit, the large closed storage space at the right of the plan could be converted into a kitchenette at one end and a bathroom at the other, and the alcove in the large room could be turned into a closet.

All in all, this building has possibilities far beyond its initial use for storage alone, and these should certainly be kept in mind when planning it so that later remodeling can be done easily and economically. Perhaps the most important thing to attend to, if future uses such as those suggested in the preceding paragraph are planned, is that pipes should be put in at the time the foundation and slab are poured; this is called "stubbing in" by plumbers. Wiring for future outlets should also be placed between the studs if the interior is finished with gypsum board walls. Both plumbing and lighting fixtures can be installed later, but by providing facilities for these additions while the building is under construction, you will save much work later on.

If the building is to be used as a storage and general utility building and perhaps as a child's playroom or a teen-ager's hobby room, the construction should give you little trouble. Estimated construction time is twenty-five to thirty hours, if interior finish is not added.

FIRST STEPS

Establish the foundation lines and level as detailed in Chapter Three. As this building will have a perimeter foundation and a concrete slab floor, the entire area within its perimeter must be leveled. This can be done by using a plumb bob from the batter board lines; see Chapter Three

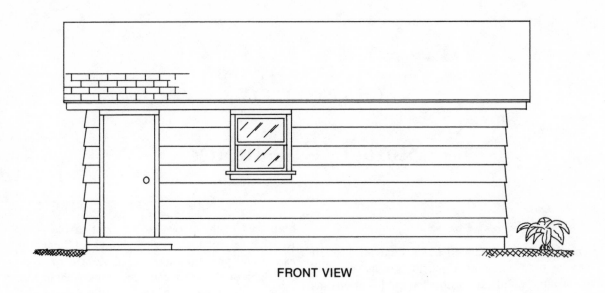

FRONT VIEW

Fig. 48. General Utility/Storage Building, front and side views.

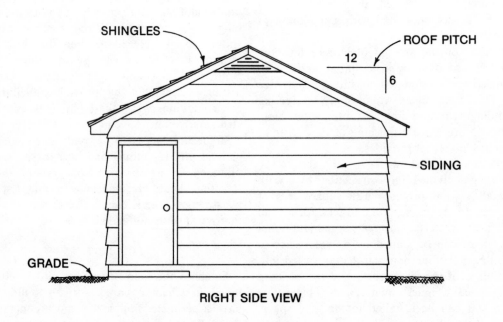

SHINGLES

ROOF PITCH

12

6

SIDING

GRADE

RIGHT SIDE VIEW

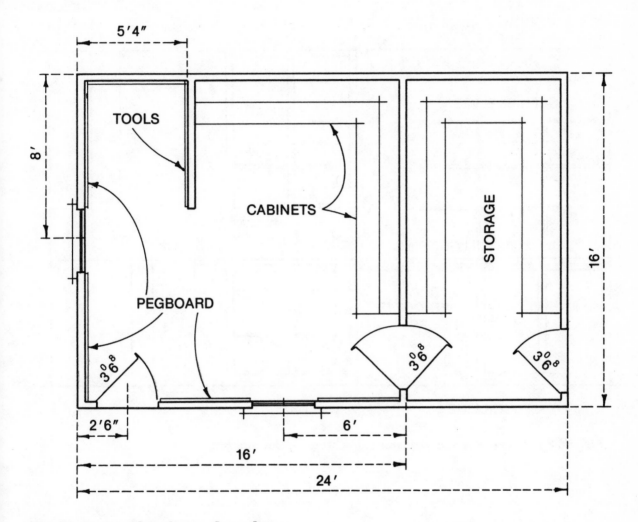

Fig. 49. Storage/Guesthouse, floor plan.

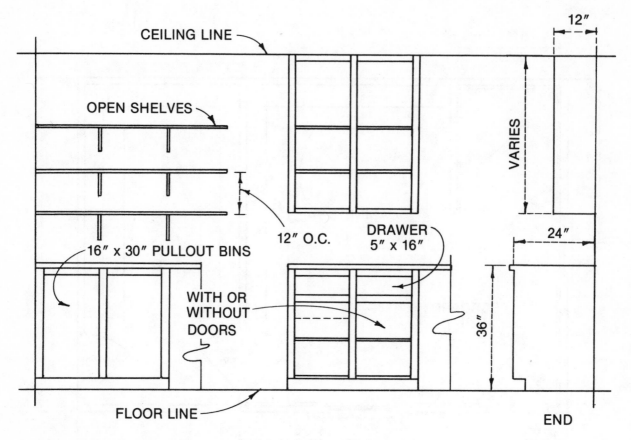

CEILING LINE

OPEN SHELVES

12" O.C.

16" x 30" PULLOUT BINS

DRAWER
5" x 16"

WITH OR
WITHOUT
DOORS

12"

VARIES

24"

36"

FLOOR LINE

END

Fig. 50. Suggested cabinet arrangement for Storage/Guesthouse.

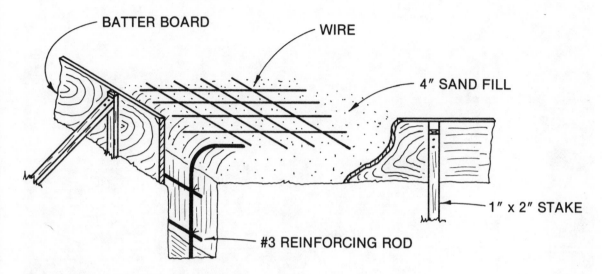

BATTER BOARD

WIRE

4″ SAND FILL

1″ x 2″ STAKE

#3 REINFORCING ROD

Fig. 51. **Cutaway showing trenching, fill, and other features of a slab floor. See the text for more complete details.**

for method of establishing a level line. After leveling, dig the trench for the foundation; it should extend 18″ below the ground line.

After you have dug the foundation footing trench, drive lengths of reinforcing bar into the ground along its center line at 4′ intervals. The upper ends of the bars may be bent as shown in Fig. 51 so that they will protrude into the floor area and the wire mesh reinforcement can be tied to them, or the wire can simply be pulled into the trench and attached to the bars (Fig. 52). Two longitudinal courses of reinforcing bar should also be wired to the vertical bars in the foundation trench. If plumbing is to be installed, con-

nections should be put through the foundation footing trench to extend above the floor.

Make forms for the perimeter from No. 3 common 1″ × 8″ boards. The forms should be held in place by 2″ × 4″ stakes nailed to them at 3′ to 4′ intervals (Fig. 53). Use the batter boards to level the forms and fill any gaps underneath them with packed earth. A sand fill 3″ to 4″ deep is then spread over the floor area. For ease in handling the mesh reinforcement, cut it into strips about 4′ to 5′ wide, lay the strips on the sand fill with their edges overlapped and hold the mesh together with twisted wires.

Fig. 52. Here is a corner of the forms set for
a slab floor to be poured. Note that the reinforcing mesh extends past the reinforcing
bars and is tied to them. The mesh and bars
inhibit cracks from developing.

Fig. 53. Bracing for the side boards of a
form should be placed approximately as
shown to prevent the form boards from bow-
ing outward from the weight of the concrete
pressing against them.

POURING CONCRETE

Wet down the trench, forms, and sand fill before the concrete is poured. Have four or five anchor bolts ready to embed in the footing trench at intervals of 4' to 6' (Fig. 54). When embedding these bolts, avoid putting a bolt in a spot where a door will be placed.

Before the concrete is poured, improvise a float with which to smooth the fresh concrete. Cut off the end of a 12' length of 1" × 6" at an angle and nail a piece of ¾" plywood about 8" × 16" to the slanted end.

Normally, when concrete is being poured for a combination of footing and slab, the trench is filled first. Have a shovel and hoe on hand to help distribute the concrete as it flows onto the

slab. When the pouring has been finished, use the float to level and smooth the slab surface (Fig. 55). Allow the forms to be slighty overfilled rather than underfilled; it's easier to scrape off high spots than to fill them in. Establish the floor level with lengths of cord stretched across the tops of the forms. Be sure to embed the anchor bolts as the pour nears its final stages. There should be two or three embedded bolts with which to anchor the full wall and two for the short partition.

Keep working with the float until the slab is completely level. Allow the surface of the concrete to harden and sprinkle it gently with water before spreading gunnysacks over it to help the curing process. Moisten the gunnysacks each morning and evening while the slab cures. This

Fig. 54. **When setting anchor bolts in freshly poured concrete footings, be sure they are vertical, and leave the nuts on the bolts to prevent the threads from being clogged with concrete.**

Fig. 55. Floating, which means smoothing the surface of a slab floor, is the most important finishing step. While the cement worker pictured is using a factory-made float, a float for a small single job can be made from a 2″ × 4″ with a 1″ × 6″ or 1″ × 8″ nailed to its end.

will take three or four days, depending on the temperature and humidity. Don't confuse curing with hardening or setting. The surface of the concrete will set overnight, in roughly ten to twelve hours, but the curing, which gives concrete its strength, requires at least seventy-two to ninety-six hours. Even though the surface will be hard enough to walk on in thirty-six to forty-eight hours, curing is not completed for another thirty-six to forty-eight hours.

FRAMING

When the slab is completely cured, carry out the steps given in Chapter Three to frame the building. To summarize: run a band of sealant—roofing compound—around the footings and place the sills. No floor header is required for a slab floor building. Use No. 2 common 2" × 4" lumber for the sills and nail the studding directly to the sill boards. If you prefer the easier-to-handle sole plate-stud-top plate assembly, which is easier for one person to handle when putting into position, you will wind up with a doubled sole plate. There's nothing at all wrong with this, but it's more economical to toenail the studs to the sill, then put on the lower plate by nailing through it to the studs, and then add the second top plate. Frame the perimeter first, leave the wall and partition framing until the ceiling joists have been placed.

Install the ceiling joists on 24" centers, using No. 2 common 2" × 4" lumber. Later you can add nailers at right angles to these joists to take care of the ceiling panelboards.

Next come the rafters. Make these of No. 2 common 2" × 6" lumber and notch them where they rest on the top plates, as detailed in Chapter Three. Then go on to the roof decking, the sheathing, and siding, and finally to the roof covering. All these jobs are explained in Chapter Three.

FINISHING

For a yard building of the type we're now discussing, and especially one which has so many alternative uses, finishing the interior is certainly advisable. Your first job is to build studs for the wall shown on the right-hand side of the plans (Fig. 49), then for the partition on the opposite side. First cut the sole plates, of No. 2 common

2" × 4" lumber, mark them for drilling by placing them on the anchor bolts and tapping over the bolts with a hammer, then drill with a bit about ¼" larger in diameter than the bolts. The extra size of the holes will give you a margin of error that enables you to assemble the studding before placing it rather than setting the sole plate and then toenailing the studs and top plate in position.

For the 8' ceiling, your studs should be cut 7'9" long, the ceiling height minus the thickness of the 2" × 4" sole and the top plates. These plates will be 12' long, or roughly the width of the building minus the width of the door opening. You will build a very narrow stud assembly to go against the front wall on the other side of the door opening. When the wall partition is assembled, with the studding nailed in on 24" centers, slide it into contact with the anchor bolts. Lift the assembly by the top plate, allowing the predrilled holes in the sole plate to slip over the anchor bolts. Tap the top plate into place, using a pad of scrap lumber to pound on with your hammer instead of hitting the upper top plate and marring it. This could make the installation of the wall panels uneven.

Align the studding vertically with a spirit level and set it at right angles to the wall with a framing square. Mark its position on the ceiling joists and floor. Run the nuts on the anchor bolts, using oversized washers to cover the drill holes. Nail through the top plate into the ceiling joists. Be sure the plates are on the marks you made when aligning the wall.

Assemble the bobtail end of the wall, using two studs nailed to 2" × 4" sole and top plates 8" long. Align it with the wall section already in place. If the end stud of the assembly covers the wall stud that will fall behind it, attach lengths of 1" × 4" lumber to the back side of the rear stud; these will provide nailers for the paneling. As this short assembly will have a door hinged to it, toenail 16d common nails from the rear stud into the sole plate and top plate. Make a header to span the door opening at the height of the doorframe that will go in the opening later. Because the wall is not a load-bearing wall, the header can be two 2" × 4"s nailed together on their wide dimension and toenailed to the studding. A cripple stud should be cut and placed in the center of the header by toenailing into the ceiling joist and into the header. If there is no ceiling joist to nail to, install a cripple made of a length of 2″ × 4″ between the existing ceiling joists.

Now, assemble the studding for the partition at the opposite end of the building and place it. The method is identical with that used in setting the full wall.

Your final step in preparing the room for wallboarding is to put in nailers made of 1″ × 2″ or 1″ × 4″ No. 2 common lumber along all walls between the ceiling joists. The bottom edges of these nailers should be level with the bottom edges of the ceiling joists.

There are many interior finish options available. Gypsum board is the best-known and least expensive. Its 4′ × 8′ panels are nailed to the studs and joists, the cracks between panels covered with a plasterlike compound. A paper tape is pressed into the initial coat and then a finish coat of compound smoothed on with a wide-bladed knife. Other options include wood-grain finish hardboards and plywoods with face veneers of real hardwoods. Some kinds of these panels are nailed to the studs, others are slipped into matching metal moldings that have been nailed to the studs. All of them are easy to put up, and you'll have to make your own selection from the array available.

Only one job remains: fitting windows and doors. If you follow the route suggested earlier and use preframed door and window units, your job is greatly simplified. All that you need to do is to provide openings of the correct size and slip the units into position.

BILL OF MATERIALS:

Foundation:

    4 yards sand or gravel (fill under slab)
    9 yards concrete (footings and slab floors)
175′ reinforcing bar (footings reinforcing)
100′ roll 4′ chicken wire or mesh (slab reinforcing)
  24 6″ anchor bolts
  85′ 1″ × 6″ or 1″ × 8″ form lumber

Framing:

  5 2″ × 6″ 16′ (sills)
35 2″ × 6″ 16′ (sole and top plates, ceiling joists)
34 2″ × 4″   8′ (studs)
24 2″ × 6″ 12′ (rafters)
  8 1″ × 8″ 26′ (ridgeboard and collars)

Exterior:

  9 4′ × 8′ ¾″ exterior grade plywood (roof decking)
20 4′ × 8′ ¾″ or ⅞″ plywood siding (siding)
      Or use instead:
    20 4′ × 8′ sheets sheathing grade gypsum board (sheathing)
    36 1″ × 12″ hardboard lap siding (siding)
  2 100′ rolls tar paper (vapor barriers, roof and exterior walls)
  5 bundles 240⚏ composition shingles (roofing)

Trim and finish:

  2 3′ × 6′6″ prehung door
  2 3′ × 3′ prehung windows
  4 1″ × 4″ 16′ (corner battens)

Nails:

    14 pounds 8d common
     6 pounds 16d common
     5 pounds roofing

FOR COMPLETE INTERIOR FINISH ADD:

Walls and ceiling:

    40 4′ × 8′ sheets ⅜″ gypsum board
    10 pounds plasterboard nails
     6 pounds joint compound
     7 4′ × 8′ sheets ¼″ pegboard
    33 4′ × 8′ sheets ⅜″ gypsum board
    Plus shelving and cabinet lumber to suit individual requirements

INSULATION

    15 50′ rolls fiber glass insulation

If plans include later conversion to guest room or rental unit, provisions should be made for adding utilities at the time building is being constructed.

CHAPTER SIX

Garage

Since the automobile first appeared on the scene, garages have gone through several cycles and are now going into still another. The single-car garage presented in this chapter is a good example of the newest cycle.

America's first horseless carriages were housed in the barns which had originally been built to shelter old Dobbin and the equipages he pulled. The next generation of cars were provided with their own shelters, one-car garages that today seem quaintly tiny and are too short and too narrow to accommodate today's broad-butted machines. The attached single-car garage followed, and because of its nature soon became converted into additional living space, and the carport enjoyed a brief heyday. The two-car attached garage followed, but even when it didn't become a part of the family's living area, the growing trend to ownership of boats, recreational vehicles, and other wheeled amusements rendered even a large two-car attached garage inadequate.

PLANS

Perhaps the plan featured here will be your answer to the garage squeeze. In its original form, at 14′ × 24′, it will accommodate one car or dune buggy, or a boat, or a number of motorcycles. When used for its original purpose, it provides adequate space for one car plus approximately 150 square feet of storage space at its side and end. The plan's main feature, though, is its expandability. The garage as shown here has an 8′ ceiling on one side; the ceiling rises to a 12′ height on the other side, allowing for an additional 90 square feet of overhead storage.

In addition, by flipping the plan, a matching unit can be built as an addition, joining the first to create a double garage with 300 square feet of floor-level storage area plus another 200 square feet of overhead storage space. And, like the utility building in Chapter Five, the doubled unit can be modified very easily and economically to provide a sizeable guesthouse or recreation room or rental unit.

Approximately forty to forty-five hours of work should see the single-car garage version of this plan completed. The building rests on a poured concrete foundation and has an integral slab floor. The area provided for the car has a slight drop from back to door, ⅛″ per foot, to allow for quick draining when a car covered with snow or wet from rain is driven inside. It also allows the car-parking area to be flushed clean with a garden hose. Articles stored in the side and rear portion of the building are protected from water damage by a 5″ rise in the floor in these areas.

BUILDING

With few exceptions, all the construction steps carried out in putting up this garage building have been covered in earlier chapters, to which you can refer. The method of digging and placing forms for the foundation and floor slab will be found in Chapter Five. The floor in this building differs from the slab detailed in Chapter Five in only one way. The trench for the footings and storage area should be poured first, with forms provided inside the perimeter for the raised section of the floor. Stub in a pipe for gas if your climate makes a heated garage desirable.

After the foundation footings and storage floor

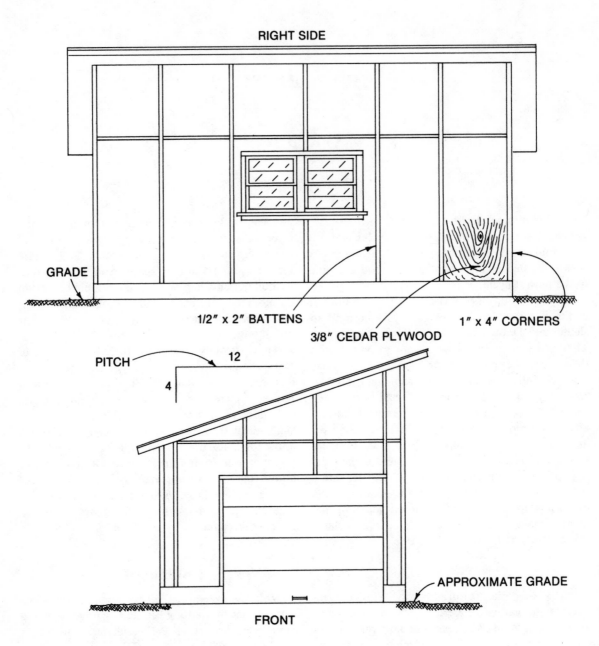

RIGHT SIDE

GRADE

1/2″ x 2″ BATTENS

3/8″ CEDAR PLYWOOD

1″ x 4″ CORNERS

PITCH   12

4

APPROXIMATE GRADE

FRONT

Fig. 56. **Front and side views, Garage.**

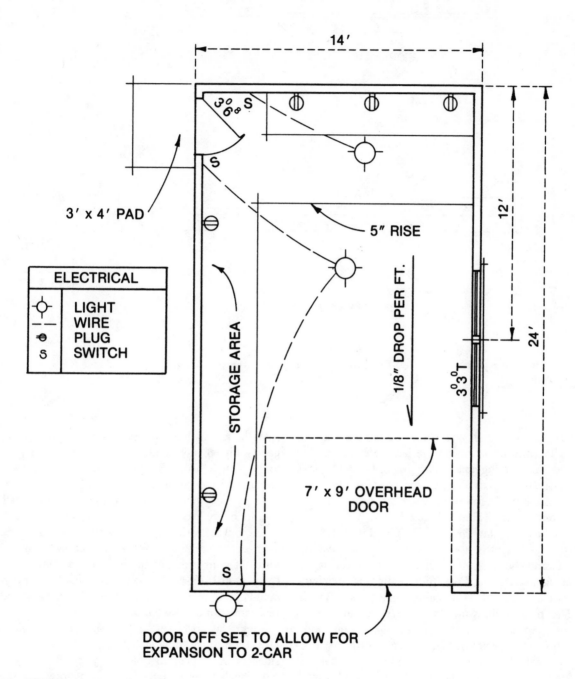

14'

3⁰6⁸ S

S

3' x 4' PAD

12'

24'

5" RISE

ELECTRICAL	
◯	LIGHT
— —	WIRE
⊖	PLUG
S	SWITCH

STORAGE AREA

1/8" DROP PER FT.

3⁰3⁰ T

7' x 9' OVERHEAD DOOR

S

DOOR OFF SET TO ALLOW FOR EXPANSION TO 2-CAR

Fig. 57. **Floor plan, Garage.**

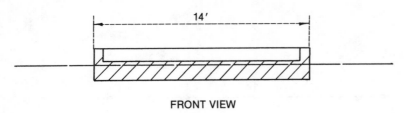

FRONT VIEW

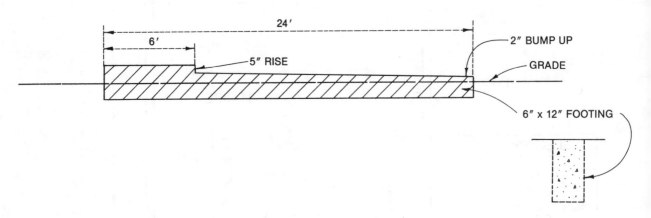

Fig. 58. **Floor pitch suggested for Garage to facilitate drainage.**

have been poured, and while the concrete is still setting, the forms inside the perimeter are pulled and the parking-space slab poured. Chalk lines can be set across the parking space to give you the pitch angle followed when the surface of the second concrete pour is being floated.

When the slab has cured, a sealer ribbon of roofing cement is applied to the top of the footing, and the sills and floor headers are set as detailed in Chapter Five. Side walls and the back wall are framed as explained in Chapter Three. The front wall, which will have the long open span required to accommodate the garage door, will need a special header and support posts. Provide for the posts when setting forms for the foundation trench. Shorten the forms 12″ from the ends of the door opening and make 12″ × 12″ boxes from No. 3 common 1″ × 6″ or 1″ × 8″ lumber. Nail the boxes to the ends of the foundation forms on each side of the door opening to block out the concrete when it is being poured. When you are ready to frame the door, remove these forms.

With a posthole digger—rented, you won't need a digger often enough to include one in your tools—dig a hole 18″ to 24″ deep in the gaps created by the box forms. Set a 4″ × 4″ post 8′ long in each hole on 9′2″ centers. These posts should be redwood or treated pine, as they will be in contact with the earth and subject to attack from decay-creating moisture as well as from termites, if your area has these wood-chewing pests. Only redwood or treated (chemically impregnated) lumber is immune to termite attacks and resistant to moisture damage.

Align the posts vertically with the spirit level. Use temporary diagonal braces nailed to two sides of each post to hold the posts in place as you check their vertical trueness by pressing the level to all four sides and making any adjustments required (Fig. 59). When the posts are positioned, mix sacked ready-to-mix concrete and fill the holes, bringing the concrete up to the floor level. Let the concrete cure thoroughly.

To span the 9′ garage door opening, you'll need a special header. You have two alternatives.

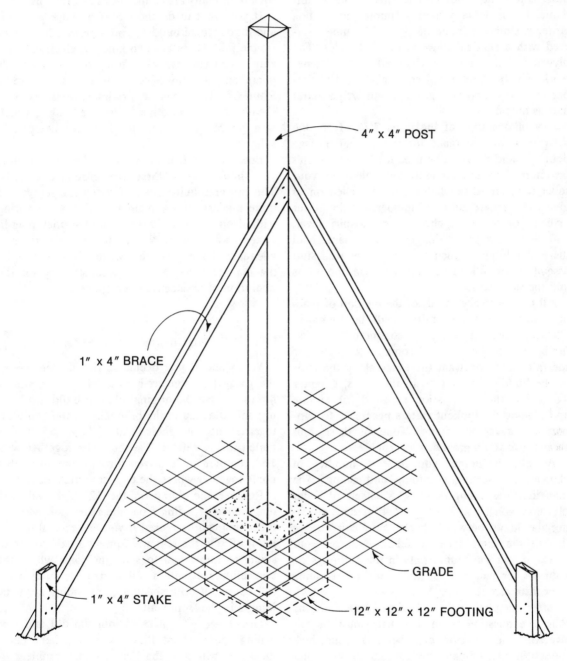

4″ x 4″ POST

1″ x 4″ BRACE

GRADE

1″ x 4″ STAKE

12″ x 12″ x 12″ FOOTING

Fig. 59. **Bracing required for post supporting garage door girder.**

One is to cross the span with a heavy timber, 4" × 10" or 4" × 12", spiked to the tops of the posts or held in place with metal T-plates. The other is to build a box girder. This sounds formidable, but is actually a very simple job. A box girder is simply a frame of 2" × 4" lumber covered with a skin of plywood on both sides. The plywood skin is glued and nailed to the framework. The box girder will equal a 4" × 12" timber in rigidity and strength and will weigh about half as much.

Saw off the tops of the posts 7'12" from the floor to allow clearance for the 7' high garage door. A handsaw must be used for this job. Don't be tempted to use an extra-long blade in your saber saw, for these blades can't be relied on to give you a square cut in 4" lumber. Set the girder or beam on the posts, check it with a spirit level, and shim with cedar shingles if necessary. Nail the girder in place, then cut your front wall stud assemblies to fill the spaces between the posts and the side walls.

All the necessary details of the method of placing ceiling joists and rafters will be found in Chapter Three. Use No. 2 common 2" × 4" lumber for the joists, No. 2 common 2" × 6" for the rafters. If you want the eaves along the ends of the building, as shown in the plans, Chapter Three has the information required for cutting and placing the lookout rafters necessary to support the eaves' overhang. None of these jobs should give you a great deal of trouble.

As already noted, you have a number of choices in selecting sheathing and siding. The plan indicates siding of 4' × 8' sheets of cedar plywood with 1" × 2" or 1" × 4" battens covering the joints between sheets. You can change this to the same type of siding used on your house, if you want uniformity in the buildings on your lot, or you can substitute any other siding your taste dictates.

After completing the siding and roof covering jobs, the question of interior trim must be answered. The interior can be left unfinished, though in cold climates both insulation and interior wall covering are desirable. Before you finish the interior, the electric wiring should be placed.

Check your local building codes for requirements before you begin this job. They may require that electric installations be made by a licensed electrician; in many areas, the codes call for this.

If you want to do the electrical work yourself, and if your local building codes permit, it's a very simple job. There are two kinds of electrical wire with which you can work using only a lineman's pliers and a screwdriver. The easiest to use is Romex, which has a fire-impervious exterior sheathing, and the other is armored cable, which is a bit harder to install. Both are completely safe.

Because a slab floor is an excellent conductor, you should put in three-wire grounded circuits. The power requirements of a typical garage are quite modest, and a main run of No. 10 wiring with drops of No. 12 to multiple-outlet plug-in boxes and drops of No. 14 to ceiling fixtures is adequate. Unless heavier wiring is specified by the manufacturer, No. 12 is satisfactory for the operation of an electric door-opener.

DOUBLING THE SIZE

When and if you decide to double the size of the garage, or convert it to a rental unit, simply flip or reverse the original plan to build a matching unit attached to the original. Tie the two units together at the gable with 1" × 6" boards nailed to the rafters. Tie the walls together with 16d common nails driven through the studs that come together where the two structures meet.

Remove the siding on the 12' high wall and one course of siding from the rear wall. Most of the siding can be reused if you are careful in taking it off. On the rear wall, insert a half course of siding to allow you to span the joint where the two units meet with a full course. Be sure that a full course of both sheathing and siding span the joining in the front wall.

Use 2" × 4" splices to join the old and new ceiling joists where they come together. These measures will give the joined units complete rigidity and eliminate any weak spots in the merging of the old and new units.

BILL OF MATERIALS:

Foundation:

- 3½ yards sand or gravel (fill under slab)
- 6½ yards concrete (footings, trench, and slab)
- 165′ reinforcing bar (footings)
- 100′ roll 4′ chicken wire or mesh (slab reinforcing)
- 85′ 1″ × 6″ or 1″ × 8″ form lumber
- 23 8′ anchor bolts

Framing:

- 14 2″ × 4″ 16′ (sole, top, and side plates)
- 16 2″ × 4″ 20′ (studs, 16 of 12′ length and 14 of 8′ length required)
- 12 2″ × 6″ 18′ (rafters)
- 2 4″ × 4″ 10′ (garage door posts)
- 1 4″ × 10″ 10′ (garage door header, or make box girder instead)

Exterior:

- 7 4′ × 8′ ¾″ exterior-grade plywood (decking)
- 19 4′ × 8′ ¾″ or ⅞″ plywood siding (siding)
- 4 bundles 240⅜ composition shingles (roof)
- 2 100′ rolls tar paper (vapor barrier, roof)

Trim and finish:

- 16′ 1″ × 4″ (corner battens)
- 1 9′ × 7′ overhead garage door
- 1 3′ × 6′6″ prehung door
- 2 3′3″ × 3′3″ prehung windows

Nails:

- 10 pounds 8d common
- 6 pounds 16d common
- 5 pounds roofing

Not included are materials for soffits, overhead storage deck, any interior wall and/or ceiling finish, or utilities.

CHAPTER SEVEN

Gardener's Building

PLANS

This is an all-purpose building for gardeners who have neither the need nor desire for a greenhouse. It offers most of the facilities of a greenhouse at a fraction of the cost. Provision is made for potting and storage areas with an independent wintering area which can also be used for starting seedlings and shoots, thus eliminating cumbersome cold frames.

As you see from the accompanying plan (Fig. 60), the 10′ × 18′ building is divided into two sections. The larger of these is in effect a mini-greenhouse, with a large glass area that can be opened to any desired degree in the summer and heated in the winter. A dished floor, lower in the center than at the edges, makes drainage automatic so that a hose can be used for watering. It has a tool storage closet that can be locked, and a semienclosed potting room fitted with slat shelves and bins for fertilizer, potting soil, compost, and other supplies.

This section can easily be converted to a fully secure area simply by setting the door on the outside opening instead of to the tool cubicle and adding a swing-up hatch door to close the pass-through. In the wintering room, double-paned transparent acrylic windows are of the lift-out type, held in place with simple button turns. A flat roof reduces materials costs and simplifies construction. Exterior siding can be hardboard or plywood or conventional board siding. To make heating easier, exterior walls of the wintering area should be insulated; if the potting and tool areas are left open, the central partition should also be insulated.

In different parts of the country, utility costs and the costs of installing the facilities for them vary widely. Because of these differences, you should decide for yourself in advance whether you will use gas or electrical heating in the wintering area. Whichever system is chosen should be equipped with thermostatic control. As building code requirements differ widely, you should determine whether a sewer connection must be made, or whether a simple dispersal field can be used, inasmuch as clean water will be the only waste to pass through the drain.

If you find the latter can be used, a small pit 4′ × 4′ × 4′ can be dug 15′ to 20′ from the building and filled with coarse gravel. This pit will easily disperse the quantity of water it will receive and will save greatly on plumbing installation as well as sewage connection charges.

BUILDING

There are only a few features of the gardener's building that have not been covered in earlier chapters. Refer to Chapter Five for the details of preparing the excavation for a slab floor and the method of pouring it. In Chapter Six the procedures to follow in floating a slanted slab floor are given, and these will cue you in on the way to handle the finishing of the dished floor in the wintering area.

When digging the foundation trench and leveling for the floor, do the necessary extra trenching to provide facilities for stubbing in the floor drain and, if gas is to be used for heating, a pipe as well. A water pipe can also be stubbed in if desired, though this building's water needs can eas-

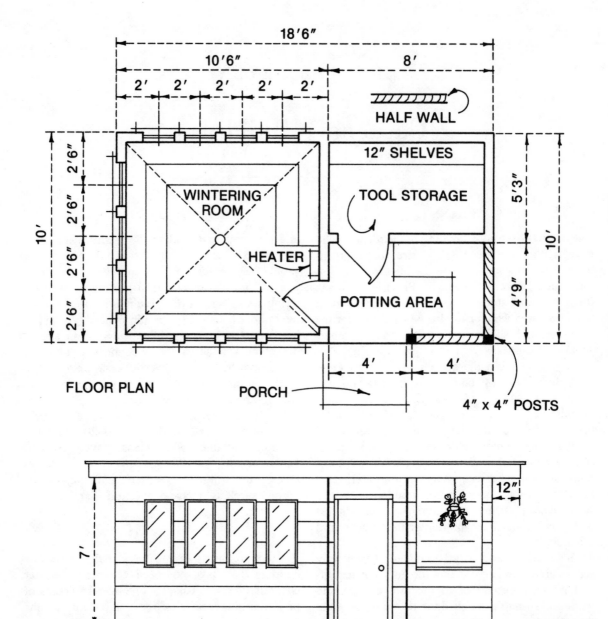

Fig. 60. Gardener's Building, floor plan and front view.

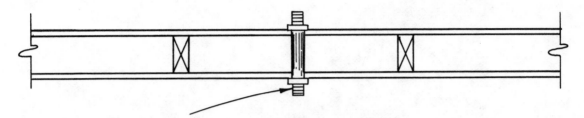

PIPE CONNECTION IN LOWER WALL. HOSE FITS
BOTH ENDS BRINGING WATER TO GREENHOUSE.

Fig. 61. Detail, method of bringing water from yard hose into Gardener's Building.

ily be supplied simply by running a hose from a yard connection when water is required (Fig. 61).

To stub in pipes, dig a trench of the required width from the point at which the pipe will extend upward between studs to a point 24" beyond the outer line of the footings trench (Fig. 62). Lay the pipe necessary to reach from the end of its trench to the point where it turns upward, and fit the pipe with an elbow to accommodate a section long enough to rise 4" to 6" above the finished floor. Seal the protruding end with duct tape to keep concrete from clogging the pipe when the floor is poured. Hold the upright section in position with a stake and fill the trench, tamp the fill well, and proceed with the floor.

You'll find the easiest drainpipe to use is made of PVC—polyvinyl chloride. It can be worked with woodworking tools, a saw and file being the only tools necessary. No threading of joints is required because PVC pipe is joined with a solvent that softens the connecting surfaces and fuses them together (Fig. 63). The result is a connection as solid as a welded joint in metal. Use 3" PVC pipe for the drain. In most building codes, the use of this pipe is allowed for water and drainpiping, but galvanized pipe is specified for use with gas or flammable liquids. Check your local code on this point.

When the trenching and pipe-stubbing is complete, set the perimeter forms for the concrete. Use an X-form centered on the drain in the wintering area's floor, pour opposite sides of the X and float them to a gentle center slope, about a 1" pitch from wall to center. When the concrete has set enough to avoid sagging and running, pull the forms and pour the other two sides, floating them to join smoothly with the two Vs poured first.

When setting the anchor bolts in the wet concrete as described in Chapter Three, be sure to set bolts for the dividing wall and the tool storage cubicle partition. Then follow the steps detailed in Chapter Three for assembling and erecting the

Fig. 62. Utility pipes—for water, drainage, gas—must be stubbed in before concrete is poured for perimeter footings or slab floors. A trench is dug under the forms, the pipe (or tubing, in the above picture) is placed in the trench from a distance of several feet from the form's outside edge, and brought up inside the foundation line with an ell fitting. Be sure both ends of the pipe are sealed with tape or a wooden plug to keep the interior free from dirt while work is going on.

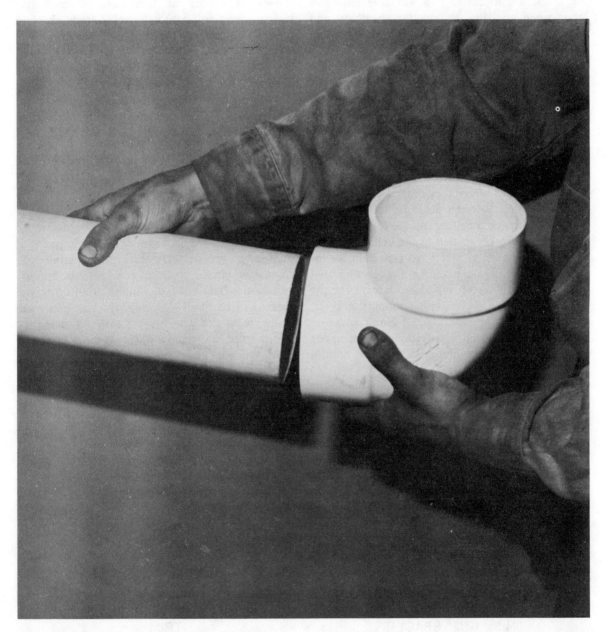

Fig. 63. Polyvinyl chloride pipe, abbreviated as PVC, is far easier to install than either rigid metal pipe or copper tubing. Simply saw the straight runs to the required length with any hand or power saw, apply a color-less joint sealant to both the pipe and its con-necting section, and push the pipe and con-necting section together. The sealant works by dissolving the surface of the material; when the sections are joined and the sealant dries, the effect is a welded joint.

studding, but for the studding sections that will frame the walls of the wintering area, use double studs between the windows. Make these by spiking 2″ × 4″s together. This will save time and labor when applying the exterior sheathing and siding, and will eliminate the need for long headers over the windows.

Redwood or treated pine, with redwood the first choice, should be used for framing the wintering room. This area will always be an enclosed space of high humidity, and no wood resists the effects of moisture as satisfactorily as redwood.

When the studding for the outer walls is in place, set the rafters on 24″ centers across the building's narrow dimension. Notch the rafters a ½″ at the points where they cross the top plates, and toenail them in place. Set cross-rafters on 48″ centers to provide a nailing surface for the panelboard that must be applied to the ceiling to hold the insulation batts in place. No provision for insulation needs to be made in the potting/tool area, which can be left unfinished except for the partition walls. In the wintering room, use 2″ × 6″ redwood for the rafters, or, if No. 2 common lumber is used, install a polyethylene film vapor barrier by stapling the film to the top and bottom edges of the plates.

Roof decking of ¾″ exterior-grade plywood is then nailed on to cover the rafters. Roll roofing provides the final roof cover. The studding for the wall partition and the tool cubicle is assembled and installed next. Sheathing of ¾″ exterior-grade plywood, tempered hardboard, or moisture-resistant gypsum board is applied to the outer walls and covered with the siding, which can be any lumber or decorative plywood or hardboard siding that you choose.

Use the same siding for finishing the interior walls of the wintering room after framing the window openings with 2″ × 4″ redwood and placing insulation batts between the studs and rafters. A ceiling of hardboard or moisture-resistant gypsum board or exterior-grade plywood is applied in the wintering room at this time.

Use 1″ × 2″ or 1″ × 4″ redwood slats on 2″ × 4″ redwood supports for shelving in the wintering area and potting shed. The working surface in the potting shed should also be made from redwood. Use spacers between the slats to get even courses when building the shelving.

WINDOWS

For windows in the wintering room, use a carbide-tipped blade in a circular saw to make grooves which will accommodate double panes of transparent acrylic .001″ thick. Most carbide circular saw blades produce grooves that are too narrow for glass but into which the .001″ acrylic sheets can be fitted very readily. The panes are easily cut to size with a saber saw. Assemble the frames to fit the window openings quite precisely. Hold them in place with oval button turns attached at the sides, top, and bottom to the window framing. (See Fig. 77.) This allows you to remove the windows completely during warm weather. Fig. 64 shows construction details.

Build a top-hinged swinging window covering from No. 3 common 1″ × 8″ or 1″ × 12″ lumber on a frame of 1″ × 2″s for the potting shed pass-through if you want to close it securely. Use preframed doors in the partition between the potting shed and wintering room, and between the potting area and tool cubicle or to close the potting area, if you choose to do so.

Fig. 64. **Detail, glass installation, Gardener's Building.**

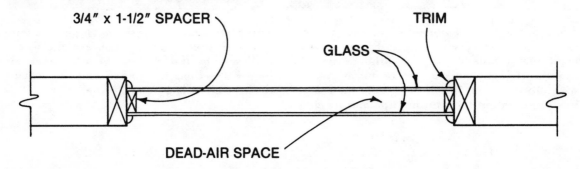

BILL OF MATERIALS:

Foundation:

- 3½ yards sand or gravel (fill under slab)
- 6 yards cement (footings, floor slab)
- 45' 1" × 6" or 1" × 8" form lumber
- 90' reinforcing bar (footings)
- 50' roll 4' chicken wire or mesh (floor slab reinforcing)
- 20' 3" PVC pipe (drain)
- 1 3' PVC elbow (drain)
- 23 6" anchor bolts

Framing:

- 9 2" × 4" 20' (sole and top plates)
- 33 2" × 4" 16' (studs, partition sole and top plates)
- 10 2" × 6" 20' (rafters)

Exterior:

- 6 4' × 8' sheets ¾" exterior-grade plywood (decking)
- 7 4' × 8' sheets ¾" or ⅞" plywood siding (walls)
  Or use instead:
  - 7 4' × 8' sheets ⅜" exterior-grade particleboard (sheathing)
- 26 1" × 12" redwood or hardboard lap siding
- 1 50' roll composition roofing
- 1 100' roll tar paper (vapor barrier, roof underlay)

Interior:

- 3 4' × 8' sheets aluminum-backed gypsum board (ceiling)
- 8 4' × 8' sheets ¾" redwood-face plywood siding (walls)
- 2" × 4" and 1" × 4" redwood as required for shelving

Trim and finish:

- 16 1" × 4" 16' redwood (corner battens and window frames)
- 6 36" × 54" sheets .001" transparent acrylic (window panes)
- 2 3' × 6'6" prehung doors

Insulation:

- 2 50' rolls fiber glass batting

Nails:

- 12 pounds 8d common (if redwood is used, 6 pounds should be rustproof)
- 4 pounds 16d common
- 3 pounds roofing
- 2 pounds plasterboard

CHAPTER EIGHT

Workshop

PLANS

Nothing brings as bright a gleam into the eyes of a home craftsman as does the thought of having a workshop. Most members of the do-it-yourself fraternity work in corners of garages or in the open. They're chronically plagued by having only tiny, cluttered closets or cubbyholes in which to keep their tools, and their supplies must be left outdoors piled against a fence, subject to damage by the weather.

If your dream is of having a roomy, year-round workshop, with plenty of space for working and organized storage for tools and materials, here's a plan that will help you make that dream come true.

In a compact area of 12′ × 16′, the workshop shown in this set of plans is small enough to save steps, but big enough to accommodate a few bench tools if you work in wood, a lathe and a welding outfit if your interest is metalwork. In fact, no matter what craftwork you follow, even if you're interested in several, the shop planned provides enough space to turn a full 4′ × 8′ sheet of panelboard, has storage along one entire wall for materials, a pegboard wall for hanging storage, and enough drawers and bins and shelves to hold just about everything else that a home craftsman might use. In spite of its moderate size, the building is big enough to allow its owner to keep three or four projects going at the same time.

There are many options available in terms of basic construction, type of floor, exterior and interior finish touches, and facilities. Which of these you choose to take will depend on your individual needs. If you work chiefly with wood, you might want to change the concrete slab floor called for in the plan and install a wooden floor which won't damage a chisel's edge or break the cast-iron frame of a plane if one is dropped. Even if you retain the slab floor, you'll probably want to cover it with a resilient material that will be easy to keep clean and kind to feet and dropped tools. However, if metalworking is your hobby, you'll probably retain the floor as planned, and work on bare concrete.

Woodworkers will welcome the storage wall, which provides space to hold a full 4′ × 8′ panelboard sheet on edge, off the floor, and has shelves above to carry lumber, moldings, and so on. All hobbyists will welcome the tool storage facilities and the generous workbench, as well as the provision for heating and insulating the shop to allow year-round use in comfort.

If the plans are followed as shown, between forty and forty-five hours will be required to complete the project. This time may be increased if you add additional features or take some of the options that are yours. By omitting some of the storage features, drawers and bins, for which the plans call, you should be able to finish building the shop in fewer hours than estimated. Adding a few items omitted from the plans, such as electrical outlets, will require a bit of extra time. This feature was intentionally left out, as only you know what your requirements are for power.

BUILDING

The workshop building stands on a foundation of poured concrete and has a slab floor. Chapter

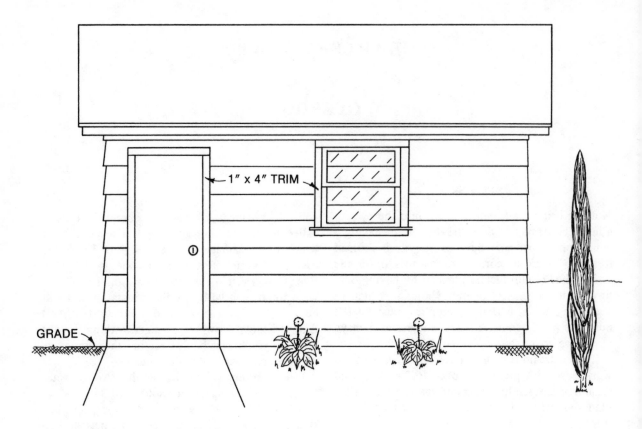

Fig. 65. Workshop, front view.

Five covers this phase of the work. Remember to stub in for gas if the building is to be heated and for water if you add a washbasin in one corner.

In Chapters Three and Five you will find the construction details for setting the foundation members, assembling and erecting studding, installing ceiling joists and rafters for both shed and gable roofs, building and setting headers over door and window openings, and carrying out all the other jobs involved in the actual con-

struction of the building. Here, we will need to devote our attention chiefly to interior finish details.

In the detail of the workshop plan (Fig. 71), the assembly of a storage cabinet is detailed, and this plan can be expanded to cover any number of lineal feet of wall space or under-workbench space, simply by building addition modules. Other detail drawings (Figs. 69 and 70) show the finished workbench wall with a center space

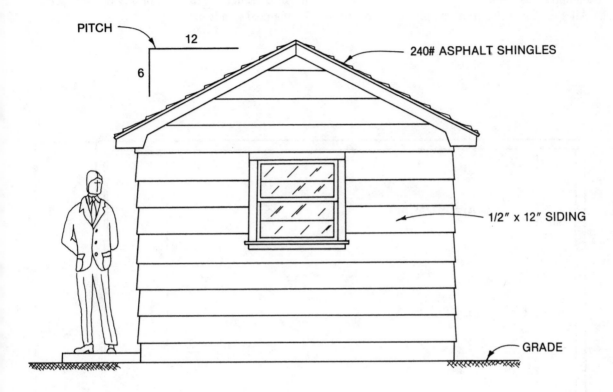

PITCH

12

6

240# ASPHALT SHINGLES

1/2" x 12" SIDING

GRADE

Fig. 66. Workshop, side view.

left open to allow you to sit down comfortably and plan new projects.

As illustrated, this installation covers an entire wall, and you may want to omit the center drawer and perhaps the cabinet compartments on one or both ends in order to get work space at the ends of the bench. The storage wall shown in the illustration was designed for woodworker hobbyists; the shelves are set high enough to allow 4′ × 8′ panelboards to be stored on edge. This detail can, of course, be modified to be suitable for other materials if woodworking is not your chief interest.

Electrical service provisions must be planned to meet your own needs and to fill the power requirements of the tools you own or plan to acquire. If you have bench tools such as a table saw, drill press, lathe, router, and so on, you will want to make provisions for flush floor outlets at the spots where these tools will be used. Do this before the slab is poured by running conduit to the floor outlet locations. Strip outlets set horizontally on the wall above the workbench can be added, or a strip outlet can be set vertically at each end of the bench.

All the details of your modifications or addi-

tions should be worked out before you begin building so that you can avoid overlooking some feature until it's too late to include it conveniently. Here are some of the modifications you might consider; all of them or any of them should be planned in advance.

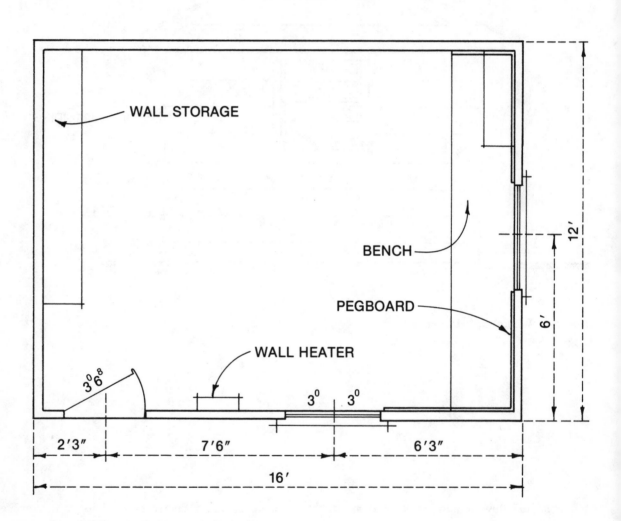

Fig. 67. Workshop, floor plan.

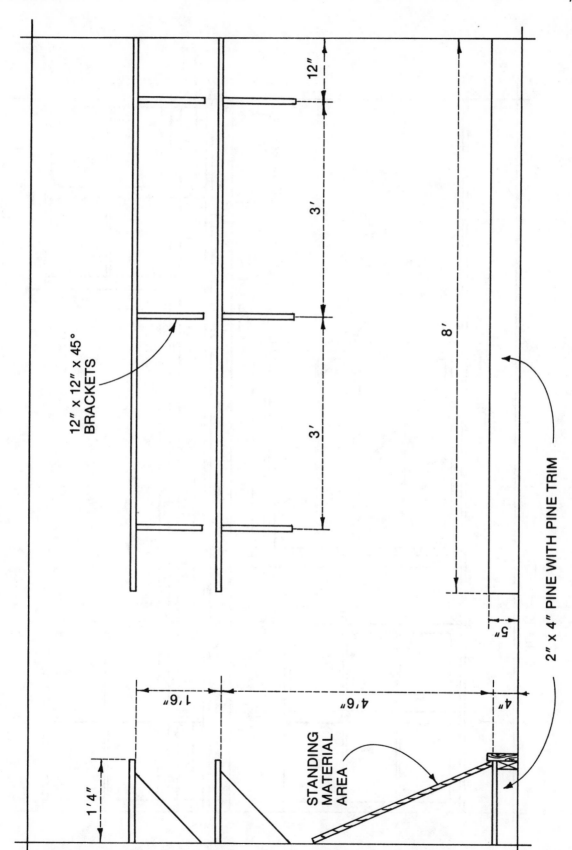

Fig. 68. Workshop, wall storage area detail.

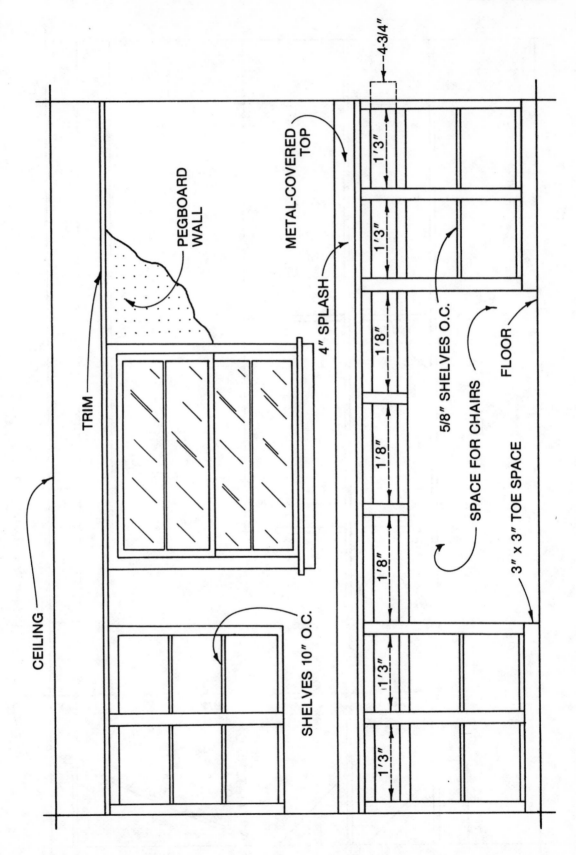

Fig. 69. Workshop, work counter wall detail.

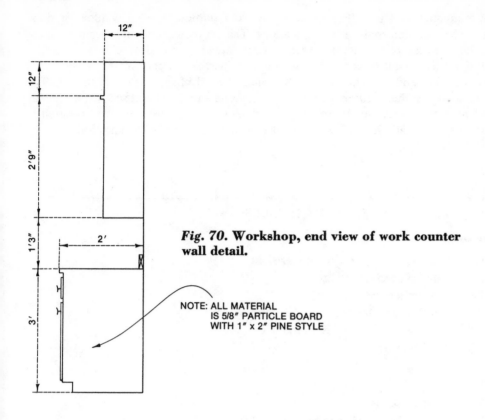

Fig. 70. **Workshop, end view of work counter wall detail.**

NOTE: ALL MATERIAL
IS 5/8″ PARTICLE BOARD
WITH 1″ x 2″ PINE STYLE

Fig. 71. **Workshop, cabinet construction detail.**

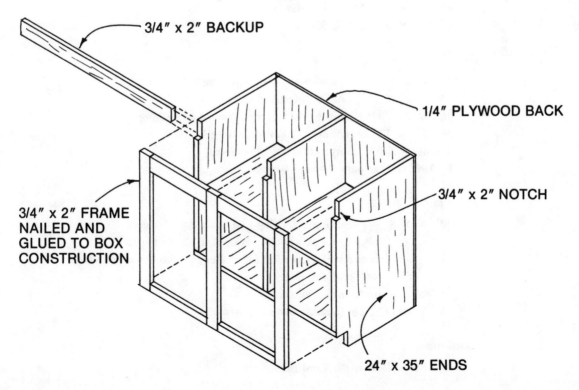

3/4″ x 2″ BACKUP

1/4″ PLYWOOD BACK

3/4″ x 2″ NOTCH

3/4″ x 2″ FRAME
NAILED AND
GLUED TO BOX
CONSTRUCTION

24″ x 35″ ENDS

Building on a post foundation and installing a wooden floor; using a shed or flat roof rather than the gabled style shown in the plans; altering the storage area on the left-hand wall to accommodate more satisfactorily the kind of materials with which you work; changing the position of the workbench; shortening the bench to allow you to work from one or both ends as well as along its front portion; moving window or door locations. The additions you would want have already been noted; these deal chiefly with the building's utilities, power and water.

As usual, the bill of materials that follows lists both the materials that will be used if the original plans are followed and those that will be used if you elect to make any major modifications.

BILL OF MATERIALS:

Foundation:

- 3½ yards sand or gravel (fill under slab)
- 5½ yards concrete (footings)
- 90′ reinforcing bar (footings)
- 100′ roll chicken wire or mesh (slab reinforcing)
- 60′ 1″ × 6″ or 1″ × 8″ form lumber
- 24 6″ anchor bolts

Framing:

- 9 2″ × 4″ 20′ (sole and top plates)
- 18 2″ × 4″ 26′ (studs and headers, cut studs to 8′)
- 12 2″ × 4″ 12′ (ceiling joists)
- 8 2″ × 6″ 12′ (rafters)
- 1 1″ × 8″ 16′ (ridgeboard)
- 2 1″ × 6″ 16′ (collars)

Exterior:

- 12 4′ × 8′ ¾″ exterior plywood (decking)
- 14 4′ × 8′ ¾″ or ⅞″ plywood siding
- 16 4′ × 8′ aluminum-backed gypsum board (sheathing)
- 36 1″ × 12″ hardboard lap siding (siding)
- 5 bundles 240# composition shingles (roof)
- 1 100′ roll tar paper (vapor barrier)

Trim and finish:

- 20 4′ × 8′ gypsum board (ceiling and wall; if prefinished plywood wall paneling is used, 6 sheets gypsum board will be needed for ceiling, 14 sheets for paneling)
- 1 2′8″ × 6′6″ prehung door
- 1 3′ × 3′ preframed window
- 4 1″ × 4″ 16′ (outside corner battens)

Insulation:

- 7 50′ rolls fiber glass batting

Nails:

    12 pounds 8d common
      6 pounds 16d common
      5 pounds roofing
      4 pounds plasterboard (for wall and ceiling)

No materials for shelving and cabinets or pegboard wall storage are included, nor are materials needed for utilities.

CHAPTER NINE

Outdoor Dining Shelter

PLANS

This outdoor dining shelter will extend the range of your alfresco eating to allow you to enjoy dining outdoors—or a close equivalent to outdoors—the year around. It provides protection from hot summer sun and buzzing insects in the summer, and shields you from rain, snow, and icy blasts in winter. In its summer mode the shelter is open except for screens. In cold weather, windows with clear acrylic panes can be slipped into place in a few moments to end chilling drafts.

As a bonus, the shelter offers a convenient storage place for outdoor cooking utensils and tableware, and you can easily add a charcoal or wood grill by using an opening designated as a window in the plan.

Extreme economy of construction is achieved by using post-and-beam construction. This eliminates the need for many building details and a sizeable quantity of materials. It also has a few optional features that can be omitted for even greater economy, such as a built-in table and two lounging areas.

Because the post-and-beam construction eliminates so much labor, you should be able to complete the dining shelter in eighteen to twenty hours of working time. The actual amount of time required will depend to a certain extent on which of the optional features you decide to omit.

POST-AND-BEAM CONSTRUCTION

This is the first plan in the book which calls for post-and-beam construction, so we'd better start from scratch to detail the methods used in this oldest of all ways of erecting a building. The post-and-beam way of putting up a structure goes far back into the earliest days when men began to build themselves shelters by lashing long tree limbs to the trunks of trees and covering the limbs with weeds or rushes or some other kind of thatch. Its contemporary version has changed only in the ways by which the building components are attached to one another. Today, nails and bolts are used rather than strips of rawhide or woven rush lashing.

Posts for the dining shelter can be either redwood or treated pine. The ends of the posts will be in contact with the soil, and these are the two kinds of wood that will withstand the attacks of termites and moisture. The posts used are 10′ long 4″ × 4″ lumber.

BUILDING

Begin by establishing foundation lines and the floor level as explained in Chapter Three, using batter boards. Do all necessary leveling in the floor area, then dig 18″ × 18″ × 18″ holes at the required intervals along the foundation lines. The holes should be dug so that they extend approximately 7″ beyond the actual foundation line to allow the posts to be centered in the holes. Consult the plan to determine the lateral spacing required between the posts.

Stretch a chalk line to establish the face of the outer walls and square one side of each post to this line. This step is very important, as the siding will be nailed to the posts instead of to studding. It's also important to true up each post to a true vertical. Use a spirit level for this job, and brace each post with 1″ × 8″ boards tack-nailed diagonally to the posts and to 2″ × 4″ stakes driven

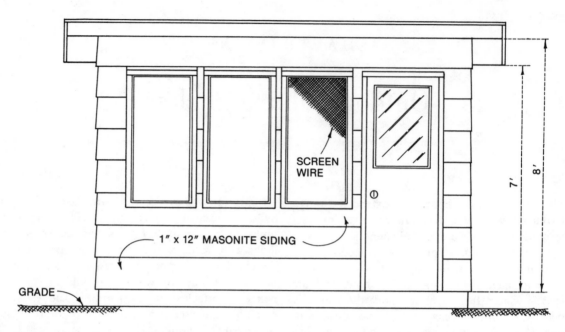

Fig. 72. **Outdoor Dining Shelter, front view.**

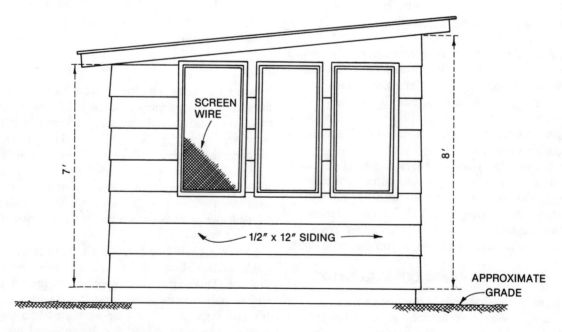

Fig. 73. **Outdoor Dining Shelter, side view.**

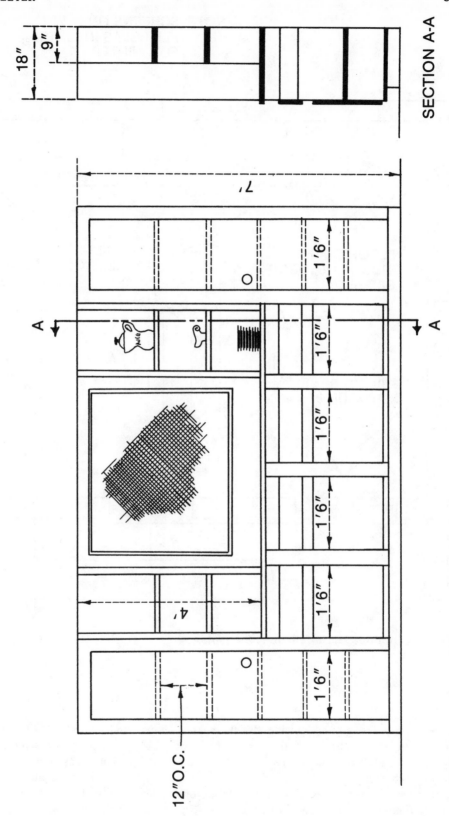

Fig. 74. Outdoor Dining Shelter, cabinet detail.

SECTION A-A

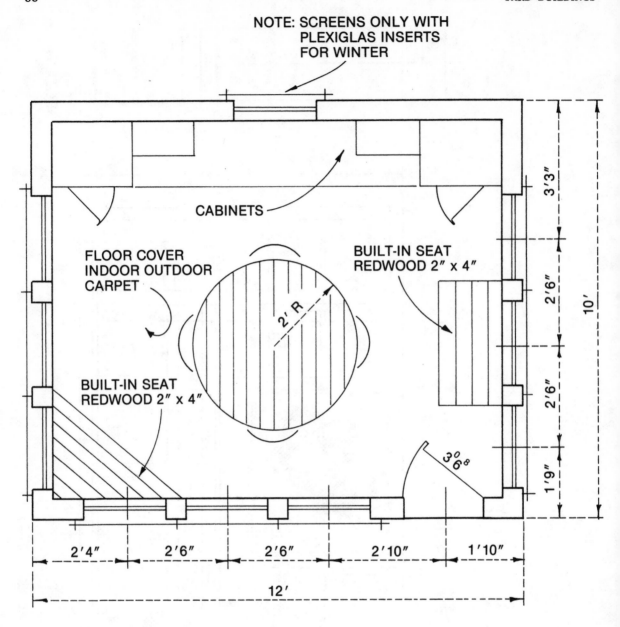

Fig. 75. Outdoor Dining Shelter, floor plan.

directly into the ground outside the floor area. Nail form boards directly to the outside faces of the posts and brace the forms with stakes between each post.

If you plan to use the fixed-position table, one of the optional features shown in the plan (Fig. 76), dig four 8″ × 8″ × 8″ holes equally spaced 10″ to 12″ around the center point of the floor area and set 4″ × 4″ posts 36″ long in each hole. It's easier to assemble these posts by tack-nailing and then positioning them in the holes, aligning them vertically with a spirit level after the assembly has been put into the holes.

Pour the concrete floor, using a shovel to fill the holes in which the posts have been placed and working the mix in the holes well so there

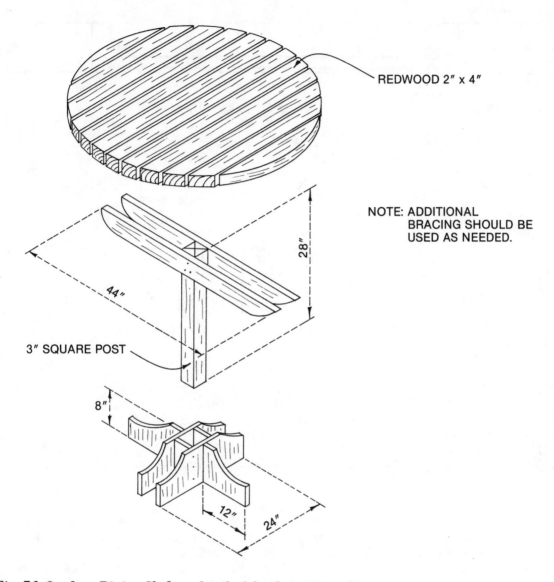

REDWOOD 2″ x 4″

NOTE: ADDITIONAL
BRACING SHOULD BE
USED AS NEEDED.

28″

44″

3″ SQUARE POST

8″

12″

24″

Fig. 76. **Outdoor Dining Shelter, detail of fixed-position table.**

will be no voids. Float the floor as described in Chapter Five, and take the necessary precautions of covering the fresh concrete and keeping it moist while it cures. Remove the forms and braces from the posts only after curing is complete.

For a shed roof as shown in the plan, saw the posts of the front wall off 8′ above the foundation line, using a chalk line that has been leveled with a spirit level. Saw off the posts along the back wall to a height of 7′. Use a chalk line to mark the slant at which the posts of the side walls will be sawed, as each post will be of a slightly different height.

Nail a top plate of No. 2 common 2″ × 4″ lumber to the posts on each wall, nail a second

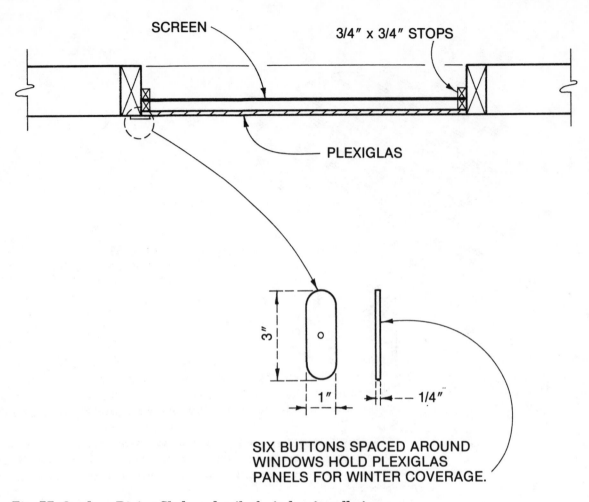

Fig. 77. Outdoor Dining Shelter, detail of window installation.

top plate on the first. While there is no need to use redwood or treated lumber for the plates or for the rafters they will support, it would be consistent to do so. Of course to save money, pine or fir can be used and stained to match the redwood elsewhere in the building.

Cut rafters of No. 2 common 2″ × 6″ lumber (or, to be consistent, use redwood for the rafters) and notch the rafters where they will rest on the plates. The method of doing this is given in Chapter Four. Toenail the rafters to the plates. Nail decking to the rafters. You can buy ¾″ exterior-grade plywood with one redwood face ply and apply it with the face down if you wish to carry out the redwood motif throughout the building. Not all lumberyards stock this plywood, so check with your dealer well in advance in case the plywood must be ordered. You could alterna-

tively use redwood tongue and groove siding, which is the recommended exterior siding, to deck the roof.

Redwood tongue and groove siding is being recommended for the outside finish because in this building the siding that's nailed to the posts on the outside also becomes the finished inside wall. As an alternative to the fairly costly tongue and groove lumber, you could use the exterior-grade redwood faced siding already mentioned. Because of its resistance to decay and termites, redwood is the ideal lumber to use in an informal shelter of this kind. If your climate permits, you can omit siding and simply tack screening to the posts, covering its edges with battens.

Build window and door headers by nailing 4″ × 4″ redwood lumber between the posts at the proper height. Fit spacers or narrow battens the width of the screening used inside the posts and tack the screening to them. Tack other battens over the edges of the screening. Build windows of transparent acrylic with redwood frames and fasten these in place with simple button turns (Fig. 77) as detailed in Chapter Seven. In Chapter Seven you'll find other details needed to build the windows.

Nail a ledger to the posts inside the building to support the seats shown in the sketches. Install diagonal braces from the edges of the seats to the bottoms of the posts. Make the tabletop—which need not be round as shown, but can be square, rectangular, or oval—by nailing $2'' \times 4''$s across the fixed legs and then nailing the boards that form the top to the $2'' \times 4''$s.

Follow the details given in the plan for storage shelves and a cabinet across the back wall for storage. Or, if you wish, substitute a grill or fireplace for the window and central portion of the cabinet wall and build cabinets on either side of the fireplace.

BILL OF MATERIALS:

Foundation:

2	yards sand or gravel (fill under slab)
3½	yards concrete (slab and postholes)
45'	$1'' \times 6''$ or $1'' \times 8''$ form lumber
30'	4' chicken wire or wire mesh (slab reinforcements)

Framing:

10	$4'' \times 4''$	10'	redwood or treated lumber (wall posts, front and side)*
8	$4'' \times 4''$	8'	redwood or treated lumber (wall posts, back and side)*
14	$2'' \times 4''$	12'	(sole and top plates, headers)
6	$2'' \times 6''$	16'	(rafters)

Exterior:

12	$1'' \times 12''$ 16' redwood beveled siding (siding)
	Or use instead:
4	$4' \times 8'$ redwood faced $\frac{3}{4}''$ plywood siding
6	$4' \times 8'$ $\frac{3}{4}''$ exterior-grade plywood (decking)
3	bundles 240# composition shingles
1	50' roll tar paper (shingle underlay)

Trim and finish:

12	$1'' \times 3''$ or $1'' \times 4''$ redwood (end battens, window frames)
3	$4' \times 8'$ sheets $\frac{3}{16}''$ transparent acrylic (windows)
1	$3' \times 6'6''$ prehung door

Optional Interior Detail:

8	$2'' \times 4''$ redwood (table)
4	$2'' \times 4''$ redwood (seats)
	$1'' \times 12''$ or $1'' \times 8''$ redwood or $\frac{3}{4}''$ (plywood cabinets, to suit individual taste)

* Not all suppliers carry 18' stock. If available buy eleven 18' $4'' \times 4''$s for posts; each 18' length will provide one 10' and one 8' post, with the eleventh yielding two 8' lengths.

CHAPTER TEN

Open Poolside Shelter

PLANS

Reminiscent of the whimsies of the pre-Victorian era, this open poolside shelter is designed to give a maximum of protection from sun and wind without destroying the open-air feeling of its poolside surroundings. The optional cupola with its weather vane adds a note of whimsy, but can also be a practical aid in keeping your pool area free from insects if it is built to provide access for nesting birds. Most species of small birds, from sparrows to martins, feed on both flying and crawling insects.

Construction of the shelter is extremely simple. Because it has no walls to pick up wind stresses, and its roof is supported on lightweight trusses with only an 8′ span, the shelter requires a minimal foundation, only four corner posts. The latticework back and sides are easy to fabricate and use only a small quantity of material.

Just as construction costs for the shelter are small, the time required to construct it is short, an estimated fourteen to sixteen hours. This does not include time spent waiting for the slab floor to dry. An option that you might consider is covering such a floor with indoor-outdoor carpet. A second option is using a slatted deck floor rather than a slab. Finally, a third option to keep in mind is enclosing the area between the roof trusses to provide winter storage for pool maintenance equipment.

BUILDING

Because the shelter will be completely exposed to the elements, redwood should be used throughout in its construction. Make the corner posts and top beams of 4″ × 4″ redwood lumber. The methods of establishing the building's lines, setting the posts, and pouring their base supports and the floor slab have been covered in Chapters Three, Five and Nine. You will need anchor bolts in the slab to hold 2″ × 4″s at back and sides as nailing surfaces for the latticework shown in Fig. 78. Tie them to the posts with lag bolts screwed into predrilled holes. Metal L-plates can be added to the corners for greater strength. Paint the plates after installation to blend with the posts.

Also in Chapter Three you will find the details of roof truss construction. You will need three trusses. Make them of 2″ × 6″ redwood lumber and toenail them to the beams. The end trusses should be set on 4′ centers, measured from the edges of the side beam, and the third truss centered between them. Joists for the roof hips should also be made from 2″ × 6″ redwood and placed on 24″ centers. Deck the roof with ¾″ exterior-grade plywood and stain the interior to match the beams. Use composition shingles for the roof covering if you want the greatest economy, or use redwood shakes if you want structural uniformity.

Before applying the shingles, construct the cupola (Fig. 79)—a simple box made from ⅝″ exterior-grade plywood, the edges glued with waterproof glue and nailed. If you want the cupola to conform to the rest of the structure, build a frame for it of 2″ × 2″ lumber and cover it with 1″ × 8″ redwood lumber. Bore holes to give nesting birds access, if you wish. A small weather

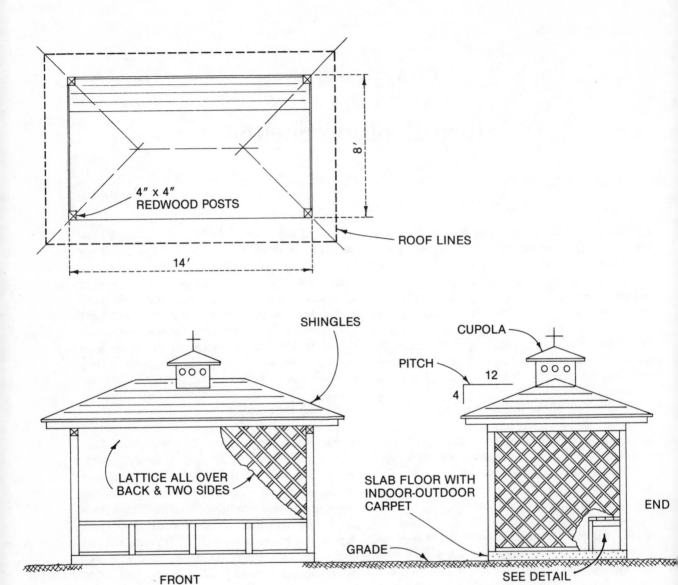

Fig. 78. **Open Poolside Shelter, front view, side view, floor plan.**

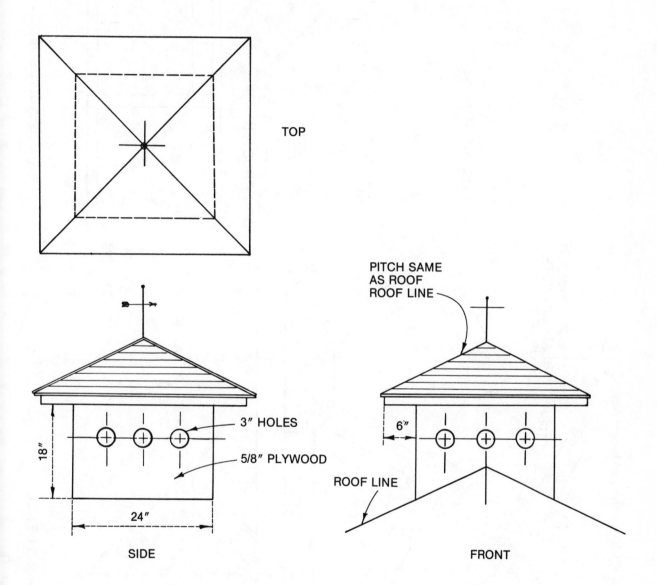

Fig. 79. **Outdoor Dining Shelter, cupola detail.**

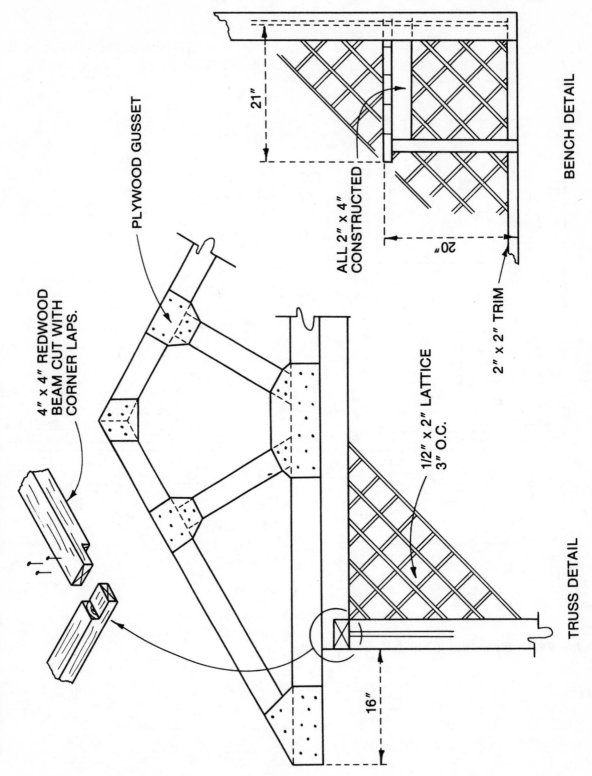

Fig. 80. Open Poolside Shelter, truss and bench details.

PLYWOOD GUSSET

4" x 4" REDWOOD BEAM CUT WITH CORNER LAPS.

1/2" x 2" LATTICE 3" O.C.

TRUSS DETAIL

16"

ALL 2" x 4" CONSTRUCTED

21"

20"

2" x 2" TRIM

BENCH DETAIL

vane on the cupola adds to its whimsical accent. Toenail the cupola to the roof decking.

Make the bench that runs across the back of the shelter out of 2″ × 4″ redwood and attach it to the end posts with lag bolts. Install as shown to keep the bench from sagging.

Weave the latticework from ½″ × 1″ redwood lath in a simple over-and-under pattern. While 3″ centers are indicated on the plan, you can use any centering desired to achieve a more open or a more tightly enclosed effect. Nail the laths to the beams at the top and sides and to the 2″ × 4″s installed along the floor line.

BILL OF MATERIALS:

Foundation:

2½ yards sand or gravel (fill under slab)
3   yards concrete (postholes and floor slab)
45′ 1″ × 6″ or 1″ × 8″ form lumber
30′ 4″ chicken wire or mesh (slab reinforcing)
4   4″ × 4″ 16′ redwood (corner posts)

Framing:

2 4″ × 4″ 16′ redwood (top plates)
2 2″ × 4″ 16′ redwood (sole plates)
12 2″ × 4″ 10′ (trusses, rafters)
1 4′ × 8′ exterior-grade plywood (gussets)

Exterior:

3 4′ × 8′ ¾″ exterior-grade plywood (decking and cupola)
15 ½″ × 1″ 20′ redwood lath (latticework)
2 bundles 240# composition shingles

Interior:

6 2″ × 4″ 16′ redwood (bench and supports)

Optional:

Indoor-outdoor carpet laid on slab floor

Nails:

6 pounds 8d common (aluminized if redwood used)
8 pounds 12d common (aluminized if redwood used in benches)
4 pounds roofing
4 8″ lag bolts

CHAPTER ELEVEN

Poolside Dressing Room and Lounge

PLANS

Here's a poolside building offering much more elaborate facilities than the simple lattice shelter in Chapter Ten. Like so many of the yard buildings in this book, it offers you options in its construction, and can be modified as desired to fit your individual needs.

You can build it as shown in Fig. 82, and have a structure with space for loafing or playing games as well as dressing rooms, showers, and storage space for pool maintenance supplies and equipment. Or, you can extend the roof over the deck in front of the building as shown in Fig. 83, and increase the amount of covered lounging area by approximately one third. This would give both sun-lovers and sun-shunners a choice, with the uncovered end available for those courting a suntan and the front deck covered for those who prefer shade.

Opening off the lounging area of the building are changing cubicles and showers for men and women. Showers can be site-built or of the prefabricated variety with metal stalls; the latter are preplumbed with all piping and a drain connection. Storage closets at one end of the building furnish approximately 40 square feet of space. One closet opens to the outside and is designed for storage of pool supplies and equipment, deck chairs, and so on. The closet which opens inside is for towels, spare bathing suits, and other similar items. Lockers are provided for those using the pool. Louvered doors maintain low humidity inside the building by allowing for a constant flow of air even when they are closed.

As planned, the building is set on perimeter footings of poured concrete and has a slab floor, but it can as readily be built on a post foundation with a conventional floor topped by exterior-grade plywood on which the indoor-outdoor carpeting is laid. A hip roof is specified in the plans, but the roof can equally well be a gabled or a shed roof. An option is the cupola similar to that in the poolside shelter plans in Chapter Ten. The deck can be built on foundation piers or on 4" × 4" stringers tied with bolts to flush-poured concrete anchor points.

If you find the building is too large or too elaborate for your tastes or pocketbook, it can be reduced in size by omitting the storage closets, or even by reducing its overall area. A single shower and changing stall can be installed in place of the duplicated facilities. These are changes which you can quite easily make without diminishing the building's utility.

BUILDING

Construction time will depend on whether the original plan is followed or modified. The building as shown in the plans should require approximately sixty-five to seventy hours of construction time, but any modification that reduces its size and simplifies its facilities will reduce this time substantially.

Because of its location and the type of use for which it is designed, redwood or treated pine lumber should be used in many points. If a slab floor is chosen, the sills, studding, and deck should be redwood or treated pine. If built on a post foundation, sills, floor headers and joists,

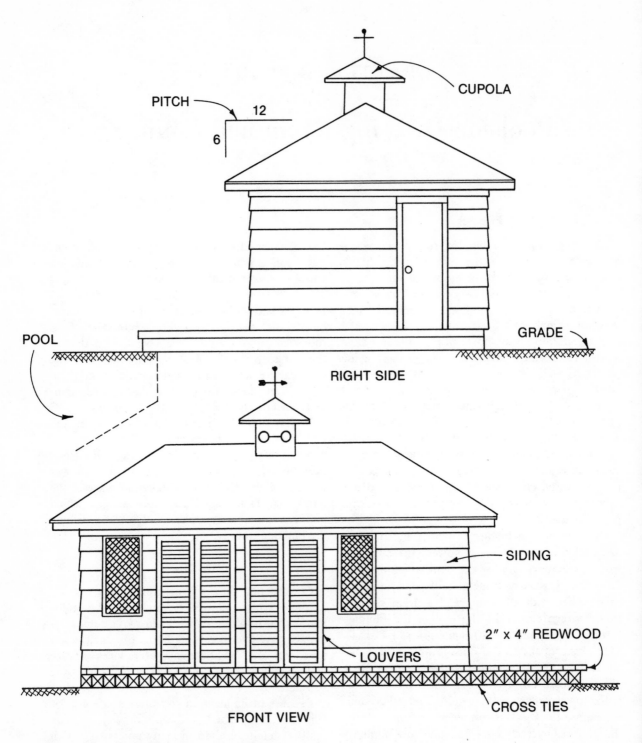

PITCH

12

6

CUPOLA

POOL

GRADE

RIGHT SIDE

SIDING

2" x 4" REDWOOD

LOUVERS

CROSS TIES

FRONT VIEW

Fig. 81. **Poolside Dressing Room and Lounge, front and side views without deck overhang.**

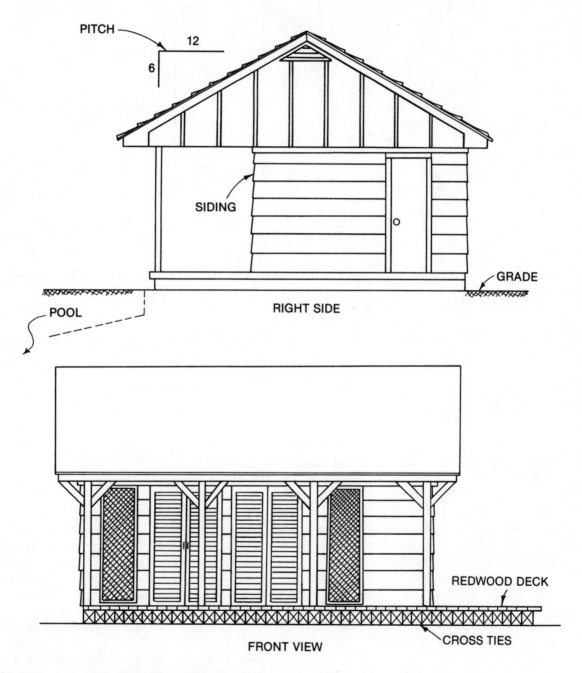

PITCH

12

6

SIDING

GRADE

RIGHT SIDE

POOL

REDWOOD DECK

CROSS TIES

FRONT VIEW

Fig. 82. **Poolside Dressing Room and Lounge, front and side views with deck overhang.**

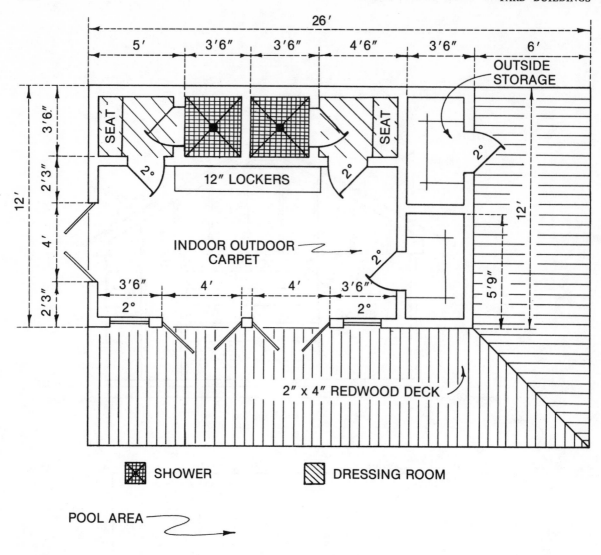

Fig. 83. Poolside Dressing Room and Lounge, floor plan.

subfloor, studding, deck and deck supports should be redwood or treated lumber. If exterior-grade plywood or moisture-resistant hardboard is used for siding, sheathing can be omitted. The use of the building and the louvered doors with which it is fitted make vapor barriers superfluous, though a vapor barrier should be placed under a slab floor to eliminate difficulties with carpet adhesion.

All the techniques used in the building's construction except that of the deck installation have been covered in earlier chapters. Use 2″ × 6″ redwood or treated pine for sills, 2″ × 4″ for studding and top plates. Roof trusses can be used for either hip or gable roof, and if the upper area of the structure is to be left unfinished, these should be redwood for the sake of the appearance of the interior. If a ceiling is installed, the ceiling joists and trusses can be made from No. 2 common lumber.

Use 2″ × 6″ ceiling joists on 48″ centers if the ceiling is to remain unfinished, 2″ × 4″ joists on 24″ centers if a ceiling will be installed. If rafters are used rather than trusses, No. 2 common 2″ × 6″ lumber can be used. Roof decking should be a ¾″ exterior-grade plywood and the roof covering should be composition shingles.

See Chapters Three, Five and Nine for step-by-step construction details. When the foundation and floor are being poured, the concrete entry apron and steps can be poured in forms set for them. Fig. 84 shows how the step forms are built. An easy alternative, though, is to use the precast concrete steps which are available in various widths and heights at most building supply houses.

Ties for the deck should be provided when the foundation is poured. These can be either U-shaped stirrup plates or semiflexible perforated metal strapping (Figs. 86 and 87). The ties can be attached to a post foundation as well as to a perimeter footing. Use a minimum of four ties for the front deck and three for the side deck stringers. Attach the stringers to the ties with lag bolts.

If the decking is to be laid in short courses as shown in the plan, the stringers will be laid paralleling the side and end of the building. Short stringers are attached with stirrups to the foundation as described in the preceding paragraph, and then tied to the back parallel stringers with T-plates. The decking will tie the front stringer satisfactorily.

If the decking is laid in courses parallel to the building wall, 6' long 4" × 4" stringers are extended from the building, tied to the foundation with stirrups, and the 2" × 4" decking is nailed to these stringers. When installing the decking, cut spacers of ¼" or ⅜" plywood or hardboard to insure uniform spacing between the 2" × 4"s that make up the deck. Use 16d common nails when installing the deck.

Construction details for the optional cupola are given in Chapter Ten.

Fig. 84. **Forms for poured concrete steps should be well braced to stay straight under the pressure they must withstand. Diagonal braces at the front and sides are nailed to stakes driven 2' or 3' from the forms, and each side of the form is also reinforced with vertical stakes nailed to the form boards.**

Fig. 85. There are several types of metal-to-wood fittings used to form joints in post-and-beam buildings. The most common is a stirrup; one type of the several available is shown here in a post-to-sill joint. One end of the stirrup is nailed or lag-bolted to the post, and the beam is pushed into the other end.

Fig. 86. **Another application of the stirrup-joint is its use in placing decking supports, as above. A second 4″ × 4″ can also be placed atop the 2″ × 4″ and toenailed to it at each side if the joint occurs in the foundation rather than at the rafters.**

Fig. 87. When building open-spaced decking, place 2″ × 4″ stringers under all joint lines and use a piece of scrap plywood, ¼″ to ½″ thick, between each of the courses of decking to assure that the space between the deck 2″ × 4″s will be uniform. *Photo courtesy Western Wood Products Association.*

BILL OF MATERIALS:

Foundation:

4	yards sand or gravel (fill under slab)
4	yards concrete (footings and floor)
60′	1″ × 6″ or 1″ × 8″ form lumber
120′	reinforcing bar (footings)
75′	4′ chicken wire or mesh (slab reinforcing)
26	6″ anchor bolts

Plumbing (installed with foundation and slab):

30′	3″	PVC pipe (stubbing drain from showers)
2	3″	PVC elbows
10′	¾″	galvanized pipe or copper tubing
2	¾″	galvanized elbows (or copper elbows for tubing)

Framing:

18	2″ × 4″	12′	(sole and top plates)
30	2″ × 4″	16′	(studding)
6	2″ × 4″	10′	(trusses)
1	4′ × 8′	½″ or ⅝″ plywood (gussets)
8	2″ × 4″	12′	(ceiling joists and cross-joists)
3	2″ × 4″	16′	(end rafters)

Exterior:

7	4′ × 8′	¾″ exterior-grade plywood (decking)
14	4′ × 8′	¾″ or ⅞″ plywood siding (use waste for cupola)

Or use instead:

14	4′ × 8′	½″ exterior-grade particleboard (sheathing)
25	1″ × 12″	redwood or hardboard lap siding
3	bundles 240# composition shingles
2	100′ rolls tar paper (vapor barrier)

Interior:

15	4′ × 8′	3⁄16″ melamine-faced hardboard (walls and ceiling)
30	hardboard installation strips

Finish and trim:

4	1″ × 4″	16′	redwood (corner battens)
2	prefab stall showers
3	2′ prehung doors
3	pairs louvered doors
1	1″ × 12″	8′	(shower stall seats)
	1″ × 8″ or 1″ × 12″ shelving to fit individual requirements

Deck:

85   2″ × 4″   12′ (redwood recommended)
10   4″ × 4″   10′ (redwood recommended)

Nails:

10 pounds   8d common (aluminized when used with redwood)
10 pounds 12d common (aluminized if redwood used for decking)
 4 pounds 16d common
 6 pounds roofing
(Nails for melamine board installation furnished with strips)

CHAPTER TWELVE

Hobby Center

PLANS

Even before gasoline shortages and inflationary price increases began to command attention, family hobbies were multiplying and taking up a large amount of time. As their scope increases, better facilities are required to enjoy them. Many of today's hobbies involve materials and equipment that can't be tossed into a shoe box and tucked away on a closet shelf.

A family hobby center such as the one presented here will add a new dimension to leisure-time activities. It provides work space for three individuals with a large desk and two work areas along the storage wall that fills the building's rear wall. A third work area can be created below the end wall's window, and a fourth on a movable table in the center of the room.

The movable table is stipulated because the building plan calls for a storage attic under a gambrel roof. This type of roof design adds additional usable space to an attic. Two means of access to the attic can be used. A ladder will work, but a pull-down stair in the ceiling of the room will be more convenient. A door in the end wall is also provided through which long or bulky objects can be passed from the outside. Use of the pull-down stair requires a space that can be cleared in the center of the hobby room.

Natural light is provided through a double window in one end of the building and large windows in each side wall. A toilet and sink are included in the plans, together with a recommendation that heat be furnished by an external combustion heater. In this type of heater, the flame of gas or oil burns outside the building,

removing any danger of the accumulation of deadly carbon monoxide. As for the toilet, the unanimous opinion of those having hobby rooms is that this feature is indispensable, especially if the hobby center is any distance from the house.

Certainly provisions for a sink and running water must be included, as they are here, in any hobby center. Such leisure-time activities as painting, ceramics, and others require running water, and hands busy with doing jobs get dirty and must be washed often during the course of hobby work to keep from soiling the materials being used.

While the $10' \times 16'$ dimensions of the plan provide adequate floor space for up to four or five workers engaged in average hobbies, if this space is insufficient for the hobbyists in your family, the center can be expanded quite easily. It can also be reduced in size if the space envisioned by the plan is too large, though personal experience leads to the conclusion that no amount of space is too large for a group of active hobbyists.

Hobby work seems corollary to Parkinson's Law: "Work expands so as to fill the time available for its completion." Most hobbyists will agree that not only work, but also tools and materials expand to fill all the time and space available for hobbies.

BUILDING

If the hobby center is built according to the plan, whether on a poured concrete perimeter

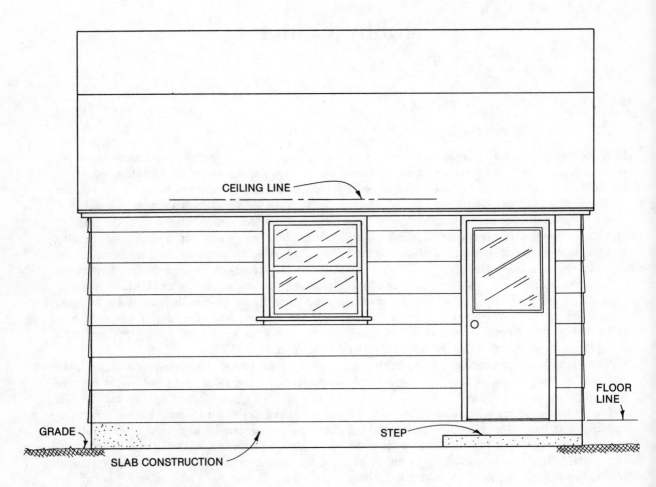

CEILING LINE

GRADE

SLAB CONSTRUCTION

STEP

FLOOR LINE

Fig. 88. Hobby Center, side view.

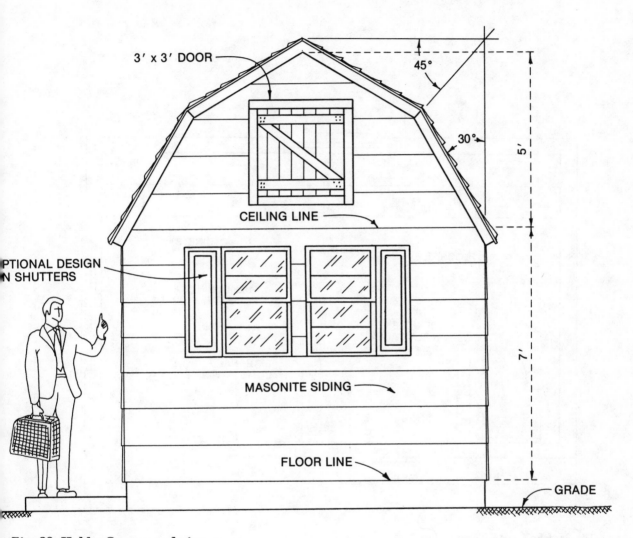

Fig. 89. Hobby Center, end view.

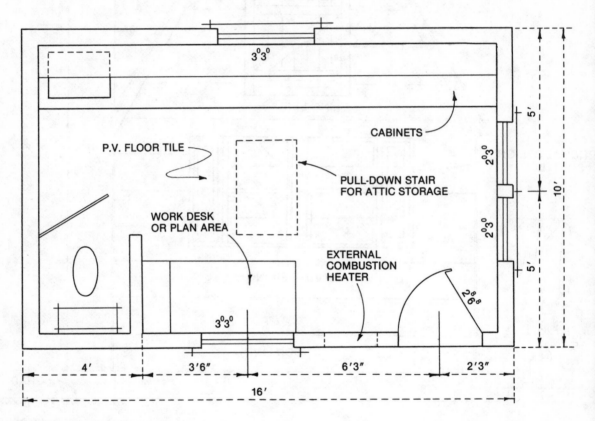

Fig. 90. **Hobby Center, floor plan.**

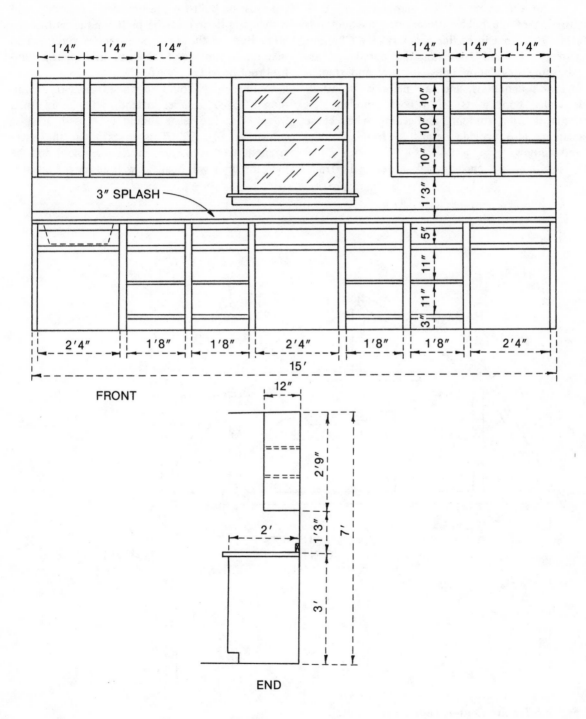

Fig. 91. Hobby Center, cabinet detail.

foundation with a slab floor or by using post foundations with a plywood or particleboard floor, construction time is estimated at sixty to sixty-five hours.

Up to the eaves of the gambrel roof, construction of the hobby center uses the methods already covered in earlier chapters. See Chapters Three, Five and Nine for the details of establishing foundation lines, leveling and trenching for foundations, and the methods of installing sills, floor joists (if a post foundation is used), flooring, studding, and ceiling joists. These chapters also provide details of framing doors and windows.

New work not encountered earlier is the framing of the gambrel roof plus the necessary modification of details outlined earlier in order to build a roof of this kind. There are also two minor jobs not covered elsewhere: special framing must be built for the pull-down stairway, and a swinging door must be built for the end of the attic. Both of these are necessary if you want to take full advantage of the extra attic space a gambrel roof provides.

Ceiling joists should be made from No. 2 common 2″ × 6″ lumber instead of the more usual 2″ × 4″s. The joists should be cross-braced as shown in Fig. 92. This gives them the extra strength needed to compensate for a floor and the load the floor will bear, as well as for the stresses

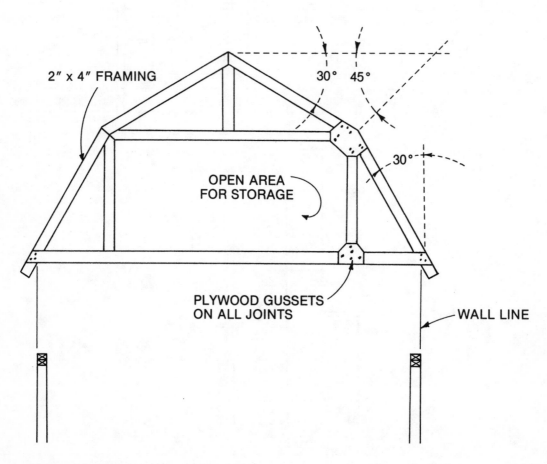

Fig. 92. **Hobby Center, roof truss detail.**

of the gambrel roof, which are different from those of a gabled or shed-type roof.

Construct the frame for the pull-down stairway with doubled ceiling joists and extra abutting joists; the manufacturer of the stairway you install will provide specific recommendations. There are several different types of these fold-up stairs, and while they all have similar features, there will be minor differences in the additional framing they require.

Gambrel roofs can best be described as piggyback roofs, with the framing for the moderately angled lower section supporting the rafters for the more steeply angled upper section in much the same fashion that studs and top plates support a gabled roof.

Perhaps the easiest way to build such a roof is to make separate sets of trusses for the upper and lower sections. The trusses can be fabricated on the ground, hoisted into position, and tied to the top plates and joists with metal stirrups as well as toenailing. Perforated metal strapping can be used in place of stirrups. When the "knee," or lower trusses are in place, they are tied together with a top plate that supports the upper roof section. Fig. 92 gives details.

Rafters for the upper roof can be installed in the conventional manner, with a ridgeboard, or trusses can be used here also. Again, metal stirrups or strapping should be used in addition to toenailing to attach the upper roof section to the lower. These details, too, are covered in the Fig. 92.

Roof decking and covering are applied as already described and pictured in Chapters Three and Five.

Before the sheathing and siding are installed, headers must be placed for window and door openings. A simple header and sill of doubled $2'' \times 4''$ lumber serves for the swinging door that gives access to the attic storage area. Build the door itself by making a frame of No. 2 common $1'' \times 4''$ lumber and covering the outside with the same material used in the siding. Put an insulating panel of $\frac{3}{4}''$ softboard or a width of asbestos insulation batt into the frame and cover the back with $\frac{1}{2}''$ hardboard or plywood. The door is fitted with strap hinges and a hasp.

Exterior sheathing and siding can be of wide boards, No. 3 common or sheathing-grade, applied diagonally, or of moisture-resistant hardboard, gypsum board, or plywood. Details of the application of each of these will be found in earlier chapters. Insulation should be placed between the sheathing and the interior finish wall.

For interior walls, use gypsum board or one of the other panelboards. A rough floor of plywood or particleboard should be placed in the attic storage area. The floor covering can be PVC tiles or sheet material. Details of the application of each of these will be found in earlier chapters. Insulation should be placed between the sheathing and the interior finish wall.

For interior walls, use gypsum board or one of the other panelboards. A rough floor of plywood or particleboard should be placed in the attic storage area. The floor covering can be PVC tiles or sheet material. Details of the cabinetwork are given in Figs. 90 and 91 and you'll find additional cabinet construction ideas in Chapter Eight.

BILL OF MATERIALS:

Foundation:

2½	yards sand or gravel (fill under slab)
3½	yards concrete (footings and floor slab)
50′	reinforcing bar (footings)
60′	1″ × 6″ or 1″ × 8″ form lumber
20	8″ anchor bolts
50′	4″ chicken wire or mesh (slab reinforcing)

Framing:

62 2″ × 4″ 16′ (sole and top plates, studding, joists, and headers)
17 2″ × 4″ 16′ (trusses)
 2 2′ × 8′ ½″ plywood (gussets)

Exterior:

16 4′ × 8′ ¾″ exterior-grade plywood (decking)
14 4′ × 8′ ¾″ exterior-grade plywood (sheathing)
33 1″ × 12″ 16′ redwood or hardboard beveled siding
 6 bundles 240# composition shingles
 3 100′ rolls tar paper (shingle underlay, vapor barrier)

Interior:

 4 50′ rolls fiber glass insulation batts
18 4′ × 8′ ⅜″ gypsum board (wall and ceiling, plus tape and joint compound)
 2 4′ × 8′ ½″ particleboard (attic floor)
    1″ × 8″, 1″ × 12″ or ¾″ shelving and cabinet material to suit individual needs

Trim and finish:

 8 1″ × 4″ 16′ (corner battens and eaves edging)
 1 2′8″ × 6′6″ prehung door
 2 2′ × 3′ preframed windows
 1 3′ × 3′ preframed window
    PVC floor tile or yard goods or indoor-outdoor carpet

Nails:

 8 pounds   6d common (for gusset-truss assembly)
12 pounds   8d common
 6 pounds 16d common
 6 pounds roofing
 5 pounds plasterboard

No plumbing or utilities materials are included here, but all of them should be anticipated and installed during construction. No slab or other support for the external combustion heater, nor housing for it, is included. These should be added to the materials list when figuring the cost of the building as well as materials requirements.

CHAPTER THIRTEEN

Recreation Room

PLANS

In many of today's homes, recreational devices have outgrown the space available in a traditional family room or game room. There are video recorders and cassette games which often make an additional TV set necessary. A disco-type juke-box or a set of disco lights may join the stereo setup. As travel becomes less frequent, home entertainments replace it to an even greater degree than has been the case in earlier years.

A separate building, which isolates noisy recreations from the house, is often a much more satisfactory solution to getting the extra space needed than enlarging an existing room. Not only does such a yard building remove the hubbub of pleasure from the peace and quiet of the home, it also ends house clutter by providing a storage area for the increasing number of relatively bulky recreational devices which we now accept as commonplace.

In the building which the accompanying plans outlines, a space for food and drink storage and service is indicated, but if this is not an important aspect of your life-style, the space can be devoted to storing games, extra tables and chairs, projectors, screens, a Ping-Pong table, and other items. Alternatively, the compartmented wall shown along the back of the building could be moved forward, and the space behind it used for storage. The fireplace indicated in the plans as an option could be replaced by a modern, compact solid-fuel stove. The half bath can also be considered optional, though having minimal bathroom facilities in a building of this type is a definite asset.

OPTIONS

While the plans contemplate a slab floor and concrete footings, the building can be placed on a post-and-beam foundation just as easily. Similarly, if additional storage space seems desirable, this can be provided by changing the roof from the gable style shown in the plans and using a hip or gambrel roof. This, with an attic subfloor, would provide approximately 375 square feet of usable overhead storage space, allowing for the area needed to accommodate a pull-down stairway.

Both these conversions can easily be made. See Chapter Five for the details of perimeter footings and slab floors; and Chapter Twelve for the truss structures used to support a hip or gambrel roof. If you want to move the partition to the center of the building to separate youth and adult activities, this is a mere matter of spacing its location within the building. Or a folding partition could be installed on ceiling tracks for this purpose.

Remember that if you decide to include the optional fireplace, you must build forms for its foundation at the time the footings and floor are poured. There are several firms which manufacture metal fireplace forms or frames. If you intend to handle the fireplace installation yourself, you will want to decide in advance which model you will use and get a set of the foundation and framing specifications well in advance so that you will be sure to have the correct type of foundation.

Most of these fireplace forms require a sheathing of brick. This is usually a decorative interior

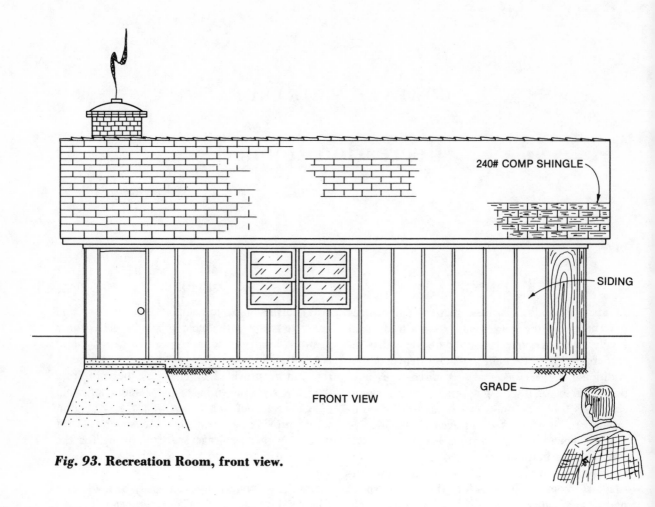

240# COMP SHINGLE

SIDING

GRADE

FRONT VIEW

Fig. 93. **Recreation Room, front view.**

facing with cement blocks used for the hidden masonry. Generally you will have the option of positioning the fireplace form so that no outside facing will be required. Ready-formed chimneys of sheet metal with insulating collars at the roof line, complete with all the necessary flashing, are available for most of these patent fireplace forms. This eliminates the need for a brick chimney.

Free-standing stoves can always be installed after the building is completed. These stoves generally use round metal chimneys fitted with insu-

lating ceiling and roof-line collars, so you'll save a great deal of work later on if you make your decision at the time you plan your building, and save opening the ceiling and roof later on for the installation. Even if you do no more at the time of construction than to include the framing for a chimney installation, you will save a substantial amount of trouble later.

Remember, too, that pipes for water and drainage must be stubbed in when concrete for a perimeter footing foundation is poured. If you in-

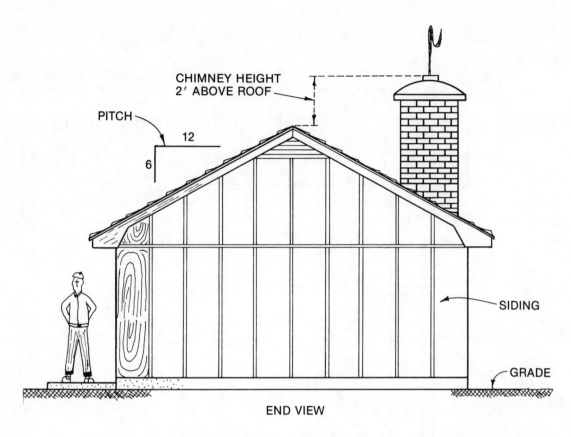

CHIMNEY HEIGHT
2' ABOVE ROOF

PITCH

12

6

SIDING

GRADE

END VIEW

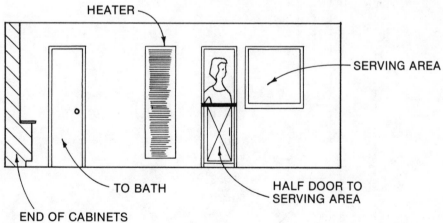

HEATER

SERVING AREA

TO BATH

HALF DOOR TO
SERVING AREA

END OF CABINETS

Fig. 94. Recreation Room, end view and wall detail.

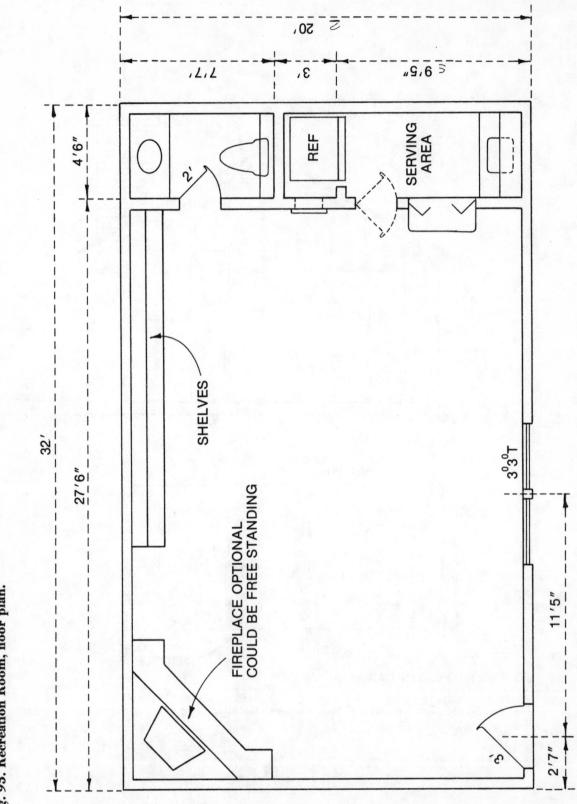

Fig. 95. Recreation Room, floor plan.

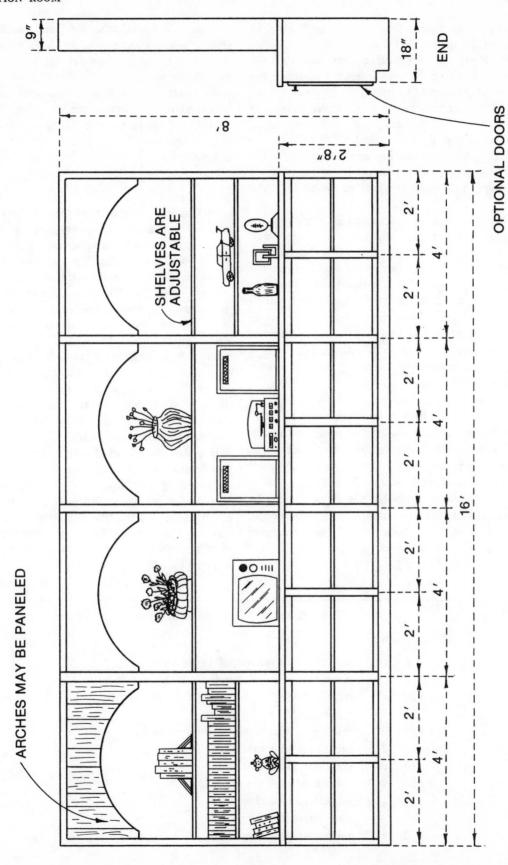

9"

18"

END

OPTIONAL DOORS

8'

2'8"

SHELVES ARE ADJUSTABLE

ARCHES MAY BE PANELED

2' 4' 2' 2' 4' 2' 2' 4' 2' 2' 4' 2'

16'

Fig. 96. Recreation Room, storage wall detail.

clude a slab floor, these pipes must also be stubbed to their exact location in the finished floor. Runs for electrical outlets and switches must be placed before the interior wall finish has been installed, and facilities must be provided for the meter box, unless you run a cable from your house box. This is really the most economical method of installing electrical service. It is also perfectly safe. You can run an underground cable carrying wires of the required capacity in a sheathing that is impervious to water and soil acids.

Hardboard siding is specified in the plans for the recreation room, with battens nailed vertically to cover joints and at midpoint in each panel to give the exterior of the building the appearance of a board and batten finish. You can, of course, use any one of the decorative panelboards that strikes your fancy. Hardboard panels are the most economical to use, with plywood coming next. If you go to a horizontal board-type siding, you must install sheathing beneath it in a building of this size.

Interior walls can be gypsum board or one of the dozens of prefinished hardboard and plywood panelboards. This is a matter of pleasing your individual taste. For durability and ease of maintenance, you might consider covering the shelf wall with laminate-faced panelboard. Using laminate is no longer a job that can be done only by experts. Panels can be trimmed to size simply by scoring them with a sharp knife and snapping them apart at the scored line. New contact cements are easy to handle.

If you do include the food and drink service area in your building, you also have a number of choices to consider. The refrigerator can be an in-wall model set at waist level over a square water heater. Or, such a water heater can be installed above the service section in the V of the gabled roof. Be sure to provide crawl space in the service section ceiling if you do opt for this kind of installation.

BUILDING

In Chapters Three, Five, Seven, and Twelve you will find all the necessary construction steps explained in detail; the latter two chapters cover the optional roof styles, hip and gambrel, which are suggested in an earlier paragraph.

Begin with the foundation, using the details provided in Chapter Three for a post foundation, or in Chapter Five for perimeter footings and a slab floor. On a post foundation, set the sill, floor header, floor joists, and subfloor. Assemble and erect the studding, then the ceiling joists and rafters. Nail the roof decking in place, add the partition studs, and cut and frame window and door headers. Install the siding, the shingles, and move on to the interior finish.

If a slab floor is used with perimeter footings, you'll omit the sill and floor header and install the studding with the sole plate anchored to the bolts in the perimeter. No floor joists or flooring are required, of course. The remaining steps in erecting the building follow the techniques that have already been covered in detail in chapters referred to earlier.

BILL OF MATERIALS:

Foundation:

5		yards sand or gravel (fill under slab)
9		yards transit-mix concrete (footings and floor)
110		running feet 1″ × 6″ or 1″ × 8″ form lumber
250′		reinforcing bar (footings)
150′	4″	chicken wire or mesh (slab reinforcing)
10′	1½″	galvanized pipe (drains)
10′	3″	PVC drainpipe (toilet)
20′	¾″	galvanized pipe (washbasin)
2	1½″	galvanized pipe elbows
1	3″	PVC pipe elbow
2	¾″	galvanized pipe elbows

Framing:

- 24 16′ 2″ × 4″ (sole and top plates)
- 235 8′ 2″ × 4″ (studs, headers)
- 22 10′ 2″ × 6″ (ceiling joists, cross-joists)
- 32 16′ 2″ × 4″ (rafters)
- 10 16′ 1″ × 6″ or 1″ × 8″ (collars)

Or use instead:

- 16 20′ 2″ × 4″ (trusses)
- 1 4′ × 8′ ½″ or ⅜″ plywood (truss gussets)
- 16 20′ 2″ × 4″ (intermediate rafters)
- 32 4′ × 8′ sheets ⅝″ or ¾″ exterior-grade plywood (roof deck)

Exterior:

- 46 4′ × 8′ sheets hardboard siding
- 106 16′ 1″ × 2″ (battens)
- 3 100′ rolls 15# felt (vapor barrier, roof and exterior walls)
- 8 bundles 240# composition shingles (roof)

Interior:

- 62 4′ × 8′ sheets gypsum board (walls and ceiling)
- 2 rolls perforated tape
- 8 pounds joint compound

Trim and finish:

- 1 3′ × 6′6″ prehung door
- 1 2′ × 6′4″ prehung door
- 1 3′ × 3′ preframed window

Nails:

- 6 pounds 6d common
- 10 pounds 8d common
- 4 pounds 16d common
- 8 pounds roofing
- 6 pounds plasterboard

No materials are included in the foregoing for the cabinets in the main room or the service area, as their dimensions will depend on individual requirements. If the wall of shelves and drawers is built according to the detail plan, using particleboard covered with laminate, you will need eight sheets each of particleboard and laminate plus four sheets of backing laminate for the shelves and drawer frames, plus nine 8′ lengths of 1″ × 2″. If you install adjustable shelves, you will need shelving hardware. The drawers will require two 4′ × 8′ sheets of ½″ or ⅝″ and two sheets of ¼″ plywood, plus pulls. The floor can be painted with an oil-based concrete deck paint and waxed, or PVC tiles or yard goods can be laid.

CHAPTER FOURTEEN

Animal Accommodations

PLANS

Pets are a pleasure, but the pleasure occasionally creates complications. When pet owners need to take a sudden unplanned trip or leave the house for an extended period, pets can present problems if it isn't practical to confine them indoors and no accommodations are provided elsewhere around the house.

Dogs—especially big dogs—can't be left alone inside for an extended time, no matter how thoroughly housebroken they might be. Sometimes even small dogs can't be confined alone, particularly if they're inclined to paw carpets and chew up sofas. Cats are less difficult to provide for, but even the most completely domesticated cats will behave badly—possibly out of boredom—if left unattended in an unoccupied house for more than a day. And pet-sitters aren't always trustworthy enough to be left to look after a dwelling for an extended period.

Here are two solutions to the problem of providing outdoor accommodations for both dogs and cats. Their construction is simple and reasonably foolproof, and their design eliminates the need for turning your home over to a pet-sitter. You'll still need one, but the sitter will not need to be on hand at all times, just to make fairly regular visits to replenish food supplies. While these pet shelters are presented as a single plan, divided between facilities for cats and dogs, they can also be built as individual units if your pet population is unmixed.

As shown in the accompanying plan and sketches, the pet shelters provide both refuge and space for a limited amount of exercise. The portion of the shelter designed for cats is escape-proof, even for these practiced escape artists, because it is covered with wide-meshed hardware cloth, and the fencing that surrounds the run can be anchored along the bottom to prevent under-the-fence slip-outs. Building the shelters on supporting posts that raise them above the floor level will allow you to clean the slab easily with a hose.

BUILDING

You have the option of using either chain link fencing components, all of which are available in prefabricated form, and in some cases partly or fully assembled, or you can build from scratch. If you choose the latter course, use $4'' \times 4''$ posts of redwood or treated lumber.

Building from scratch will cost approximately half the price of using the necessary prefabricated chain link components. The amount of work involved is roughly the same. The animal accommodation enclosure as shown in the plan, with one section for dogs and another for cats, will require sixteen to eighteen hours of work if you use chain link fence components, perhaps an hour more if you build from scratch. The dog or cat enclosure alone will require ten to twelve hours of work if prefabricated materials are used, an hour or so more if it is entirely site-built.

Preliminary work for either option is leveling the area to be enclosed. If you are building from scratch, dig a shallow trench around the perimeter of the area, $2''$ to $3''$ below the level of the sand-fill that will be spread and compacted for the floor. See Chapter Five for leveling and trenching details.

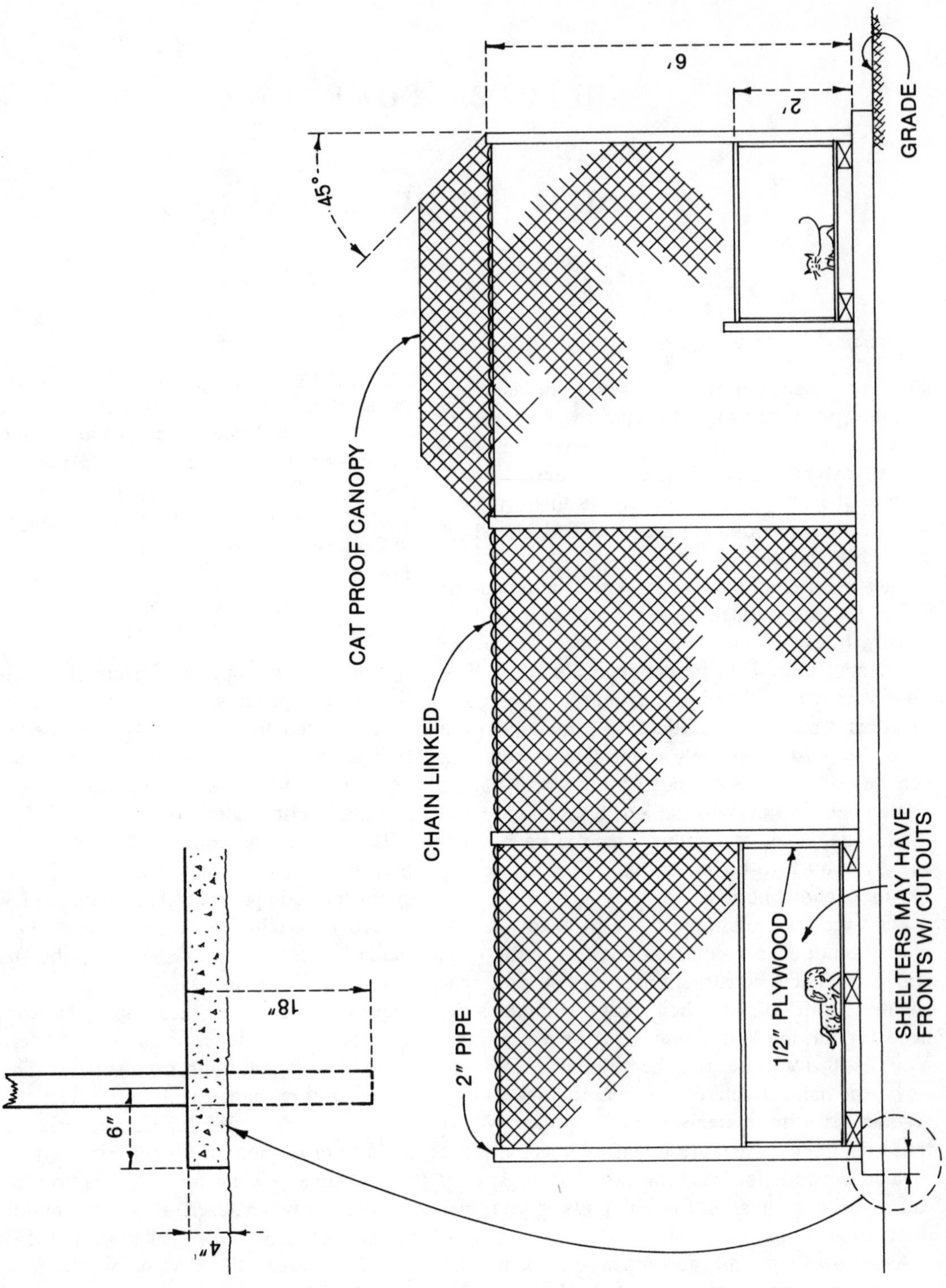

Fig. 97. Animal Accommodations, side view.

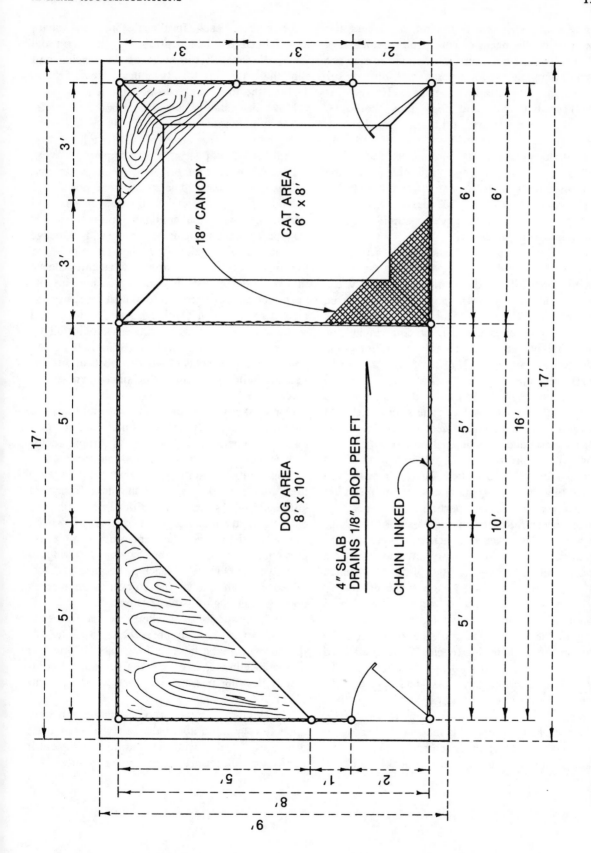

Fig. 98. Animal Accommodations, floor plan.

For a single enclosure, use the portion of the plan that fits the needs of your pets, whether dogs or cats. The cat enclosure is adequate in size for a small dog, but not for several small dogs or for a large one. Dogs need pacing space. However, if you keep both cats and dogs, they should be separated when confined, no matter how friendly they are. If you are using 4″ × 4″ redwood posts, holes should be 10″ in diameter and 18″ to 24″ deep; the actual depth will depend on the soil consistency. In soft, wet, or sandy soils the posts should be 24″ to 30″ deep. Most rental outlets featuring tools have posthole diggers, which make the job easier.

Make the center and gate posts from 10′ lengths of 4″ × 4″ lumber, sawed to a uniform length of 6′6″, if 18″ deep holes are dug. Saw the tops of the posts at a 45° angle, and square the ends of the 20″ lengths. Nail these short lengths to the angled ends and cut bracing angles for each side of each post from ½″ exterior-grade plywood or hardboard. Nail these over the joints to reinforce them.

Set the posts in the holes and align them with a spirit level and a chalk line. The gatepost should be set in the desired corner centered 48″ from the corner post, and a dual enclosure for cats and dogs will require posts and gateposts for the fencing that divides the shelter. Level all posts and brace them with diagonals made of scrap lumber nailed from the upper portion of the posts to stakes driven into the ground, as shown in Chapter Three. Use sacked concrete mix to fill the holes and let it set twenty-four to thirty-six hours before removing the braces. Toenail 2″ × 4″ stringers between the posts at the top.

Forms made of 1″ × 6″ or 1″ × 8″ No. 3 common or form lumber should extend about 2″ beyond the outside faces of the posts, and the bottom of the chain link fencing should be buried in the concrete all around the shelter. Use 11½ gauge fencing, which has a 2⅛″ mesh. To pull the fencing tight, drive some 1″ × ⅜″ lag bolts into a piece of 2″ × 4″ on 24″ centers (Fig. 99). Wrap a chain around the fencepost in a spiral from top to bottom; hold each end in place with a nail or wire tie. Extend stout turnbuckles and slip

a hook from each turnbuckle into the chain loops. Push the heads of the lag bolts on the 2″ × 4″ through the mesh of the fencing and slip the eyes of the turnbuckles over them. Tighten the turnbuckles to pull the fencing tight.

Make the gates of No. 2 common 2″ × 4″s, and staple the mesh to them. Staple hardware cloth between the arms of the overhang and anchor it to the top stringer with staples.

Fencing with prefabricated metal posts and fittings is a bit easier. The round metal posts need not be set into concrete if you use the patented anchors that some makers offer. Unless the soil is very hard, the posts can be driven with a sledge hammer—put a galvanized pipe-cap-nipple on top to protect the post—or with a weighted sleeve that some dealers will loan or rent. There are fittings such as corner connectors, post caps, prefabricated gates, metal overhang arms, and top and bottom rails, all of which are easy to install by following the manufacturers' directions. It's up to you to weigh the costs of wooden posts and from-scratch building against the time involved in erecting each.

Don't skimp on the job by omitting the overhang, though. Not even a small dog, and certainly not a cat, can be confined in a small enclosure without an overhang. Dogs can show a surprising ability to climb fences when they make up their minds to do so, and cats have a natural knack for taking fences in stride. In fact, if your cat or cats are really good at escaping, you'd be well advised to cover their enclosure completely, using hardware cloth. And beware of trying to substitute chicken wire fencing, because a determined cat can stretch the chicken wire meshes open wide enough to squeeze through.

Build plywood box shelters, and a frame of 1″ × 2″ or 2″ × 2″ lumber, set 8″ to 12″ above the floor, to make hose flushing easy. If you live in a cold climate, close the shelters almost completely, leaving just enough space for the pets to get in.

This kind of animal accommodation not only relieves your mind about the safety of your pets, it assures you that whoever you hire to replenish their food will not need to enter your home.

Fig. 99. This improvised lash-up can be used when tightening chain link fencing during its installation on either wood or metal posts. Use as many lag bolts in a length of 2″ × 4″ as are required to span the height of the chain link mesh, and tighten each turnbuckle in turn to pull the fencing taut. Then, fasten the chain link with staples to wooden posts, with wire ties to metal posts.

BILL OF MATERIALS:

(Using redwood posts)

Slab:

3½	yards sand or gravel (fill)
4½	yards transit-mix concrete (slab and postholes)
35′	48″ chicken wire or mesh (slab reinforcement)
55	running feet 1″ × 6″ or 1″ × 8″ form lumber

Posts:

14	4″ × 4″ 8′ redwood
1	2″ × 4″ 8′ redwood (overhang for cat area)

Fencing:

45′	11½ gauge chain link fencing
30′	18″ hardware cloth (overhang)
4	pounds galvanized staples

Gates:

4	10′ 2″ × 4″ redwood

Shelters:

1	4′ × 8′ ¾″ sheet exterior-grade plywood
1	2″ × 4″ 20′ redwood

(Using chain link posts)

Posts and fencing:

14	8′	galvanized
7	18″	45° angle arms (overhang)
6		top caps
12		tension bars
48		tension bands
45′	11½	gauge chain link fencing

Gates:

2	2′ × 6′ with mounting hardware

Shelters: Same as above

It will be up to you to decide, after studying comparative costs and working times, whether to make your pet accommodations from prefabricated materials or whether to use wooden posts and gates. You may also want to revise the size and shape of the shelters suggested in the plans.

CHAPTER FIFTEEN

Greenhouse

PLANS

Greenhouses may well be the first structures created by man to collect and use solar energy. As distinguished from hothouses, which are artificially heated, a greenhouse is designed to encourage plant growth the year around in a warm, humid atmosphere created when heat from the sun's rays accumulates beneath a clear-paned roof. And almost every dedicated gardener north of the tropics would like to have one.

There's nothing especially difficult about the construction of a greenhouse. In the accompanying plan, the post-and-beam method of building is used to produce an extremely rigid frame which reduces to a minimum the quantity of materials and the amount of work involved in installing the glass walls and roof.

BUILDING

Posts made of redwood 4″ × 4″s are set in concrete at each corner of a 12′ × 20′ concrete slab floor, with intermediate posts set on 48″ centers from the corner posts on each side and on 6′ centers at each end. Top plates of 2″ × 4″ redwood are nailed to the posts, with short sole plates toenailed between the posts along the bottom. Studs of 2″ × 4″ redwood are set on 24″ centers between the posts. Because the posts support the building, only token footings are needed.

Trusses and intermediate rafters bear the weight of the gambrel roof, this roof configuration being chosen because it gives the maximum exposed area. The trusses are placed at the ends of the building and above the intermediate supporting posts, with rafters on 24″ centers between the trusses. Spacers of 2″ × 6″ redwood are set vertically between the trusses and rafters at the ridgeline and 2″ × 4″ spacers are placed between the vertical members along the lines of the roof breaks. These spacers tie the rafters and trusses together.

Along the inside faces of the trusses and rafters, laths are nailed to support the panes of clear acrylic that form the roof. These panes are set in caulking compound and secured by nailing 1″ × 3″ strips to the top edge of each rafter. The side windows below the eaves line are hinged to swing outward and supply ventilation. These panes are framed in grooves sawed in 2″ × 2″ redwood; a carbide-tipped blade in a circular saw makes a groove exactly wide enough to accept the .001″ thick acrylic panes.

Siding can be 1″ × 12″ redwood lap siding or 1″ × 2″ hardboard lap siding. The rigidity provided by the supporting posts makes sheathing unnecessary. Headers will have to be toenailed between the posts and studs to provide a nailing surface for the siding and to serve as windowsills. The headers can be set flush, or the headers can be made of 2″ × 6″ redwood to provide an overhang against which the top edge of the siding boards can be butted.

A center drain in the floor slab allows gravity runoff of water. A worktable is shown in the plans in the center of the greenhouse, with redwood slat shelves along the sides and ends. This worktable should be set on short legs, if placed as

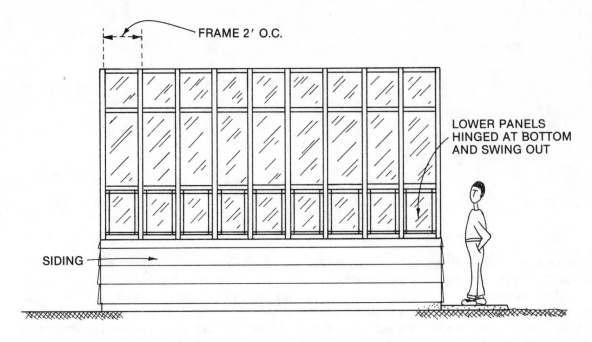

SIDE VIEW

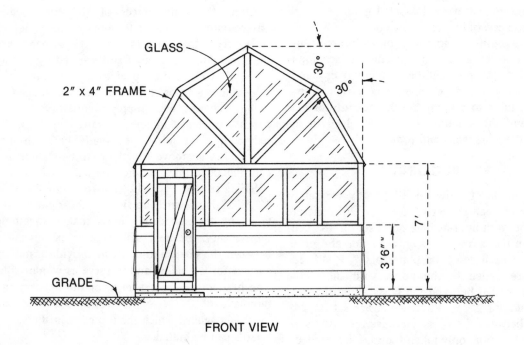

FRONT VIEW

Fig. 100. **Greenhouse, side and front views.**

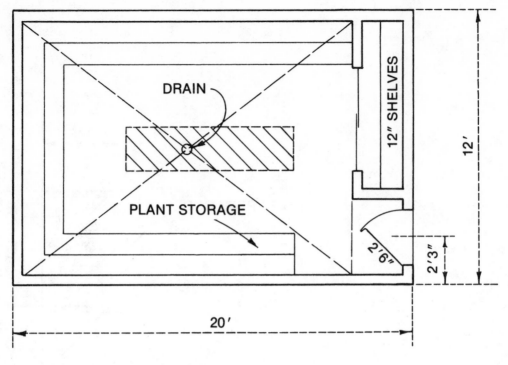

FLOOR PLAN

Fig. 101. Greenhouse, floor plan.

Fig. 102. Greenhouse, glass installation detail.

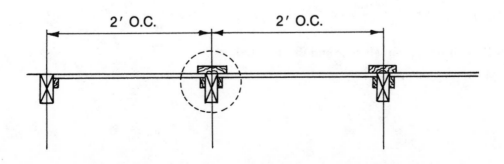

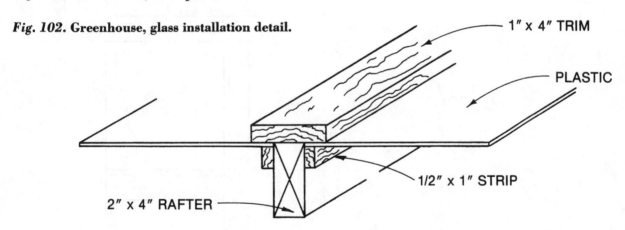

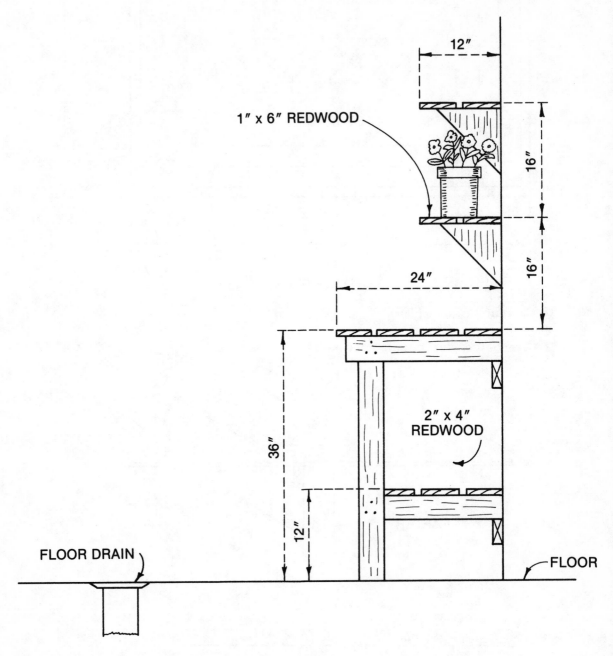

Fig. 103. Greenhouse, plant storage and drain detail.

Fig. 104. **Greenhouse, potting bench and storage bin details.**

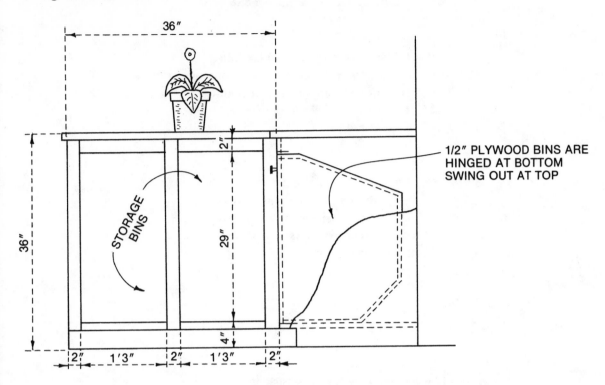

1/2″ PLYWOOD BINS ARE HINGED AT BOTTOM SWING OUT AT TOP

STORAGE BINS

indicated. Bins under the worktable provide storage for the materials used in potting and setting plants.

Because the interior of the greenhouse will be quite humid, redwood lumber should be used throughout its construction. Due to the amount of detail work involved in assembling the trusses and setting the panes, approximately fifty to sixty hours is estimated as the construction time.

BILL OF MATERIALS:

Floor:

4	yards sand or gravel (fill under slab)
5	yards transit-mix concrete (floor and postholes)
65′	48″ chicken wire or mesh (slab reinforcing)
75	running feet 1″ × 6″ or 1″ × 8″ form lumber
20′	2″ PVC pipe (drain)
1	2″ PVC elbow (drain)

Framing:

10	4″ × 4″ 10′ redwood (posts)
4	4″ × 4″ 16′ redwood (top plate)

Or use instead:

  8 2″ × 4″ 16′ redwood (top plates)

82 2″ × 4″ 20′ redwood (trusses, rafters, headers, sole plates, studs)

  2 2″ × 6″ 20′ redwood (spacers, window sills)

Exterior:

16 1″ × 2″ 16′ hardboard or redwood lap siding

450 ½″ × 1″ running feet redwood lath (roof pane supports)

45 1″ × 3″ 10′ redwood (roof pane outer framing)

30 2″ × 2″ 10′ redwood (wall window frames)

26 1″ × 2″ hinges (wall panes)

Interior:

33 1″ × 6″ 12′ redwood (shelving)

15 2″ × 4″ 8′ redwood (legs, bottom shelving)

  6 1″ × 8″ 8′ redwood (supports, top shelving)

43 24″ × 30″ acrylic panes (windows)

36 24″ × 48″ acrylic panes (roof)

  4 48″ × 64″ acrylic panes (ends)

Finish and trim:

  1 2′6″ × 6′6″ prehung door

Nails:

  8 pounds 6d aluminum or other rust-resistant

12 pounds 8d aluminum or other rust-resistant

  6 pounds 16d aluminum or other rust-resistant

No materials are included for the center work-table, as it will probably be built to suit individual needs. It should be made from ¾″ exterior-grade plywood, and all joints should be glued with waterproof glue. Alternatively, the table can be made from redwood lumber or from a redwood 2″ × 2″ frame covered with ⅜″ or ½″ exterior-grade hardboard.

CHAPTER SIXTEEN

Playhouses and Whimsies

SURPLUS MATERIALS

Whenever a building project is completed, no matter how small, the builder is left not only with a sense of satisfaction, but with odds and ends of surplus lumber. This will happen even when the materials list has been scanned with the greatest care, and only the essential items ordered.

Some dealers will accept returned lumber if the material is in its original condition. They won't take back sections of 4' × 4' panelboards, or boards that have nail holes or saw cuts or other marks of previous use, however. As a result, odd lengths of lumber, quarter sheets or half sheets of paneling, bits and pieces of molding, nails, and so on, gather dust and deteriorate. What's left may not be returnable, but it's too good to throw away or burn, and nobody seems interested in having it, even as a gift.

One way to use up the surplus is by building a playhouse or a dollhouse or a tree house, if you have a suitable tree. Other projects that could absorb your surplus material are a sandbox, perhaps one with a sun shelter, or a gym for toddlers, or even for older youngsters.

On the adult level, you could think about one of those buildings, now coming back into fashion, that in pre-Victorian Britain were called whimsies. These are structures like gazebos and pergolas, originally designed to provide an overhead shelter for the mistress of the house and her guests so that they could enjoy their afternoon tea in the middle of the garden.

A few ideas that may stimulate your imagination follow.

A-FRAME PLAY SHELTER

This simple playhouse can be built from two half sheets, 4' × 4' each, of any exterior-grade plywood or hardboard, plus a few 4' lengths of 1" lumber and two 4' lengths of 2" × 4". You will also need seven lengths of 1" × 2" lumber 34½" long, but these can be ripped from wider stock.

Make a base for the shelter by nailing two wide boards 4' long at right angles to the 2" × 4"s, to produce a platform 4' long by 3½' wide. The boards should be centered on the 2" × 4" and their edges flush with the edges of the 2" × 4" pieces. This will allow the ends of the 2" × 4"s to protrude about 3" at each corner. If you have a piece of ¾" plywood 4' × 3½', it can be used instead of boards to make the platform.

Center the 1" × 2" strips along the edges and at the centers of each of the 4' × 4' plywood squares; the ends of the 1" × 2"s should be ¾" from the edges of the plywood at top and bottom. Use 4d common or finishing nails.

Tack-nail the remaining 1" × 2" on edge, with its wide dimension butted to the strips, by nailing through the plywood into the 1" × 2". Then tack-nail the remaining plywood panel to the 1" × 2" in the same position.

Fit the assembled panels to the platform by spreading the edges opposite the nailed edges and nailing them to the platform. Butt the bottom edges of the panel to the sides of the platform, resting their ends on the protruding 2" × 4"s. Nail the plywood to the 2" × 4"s and into the floor along each edge with 8d finishing nails.

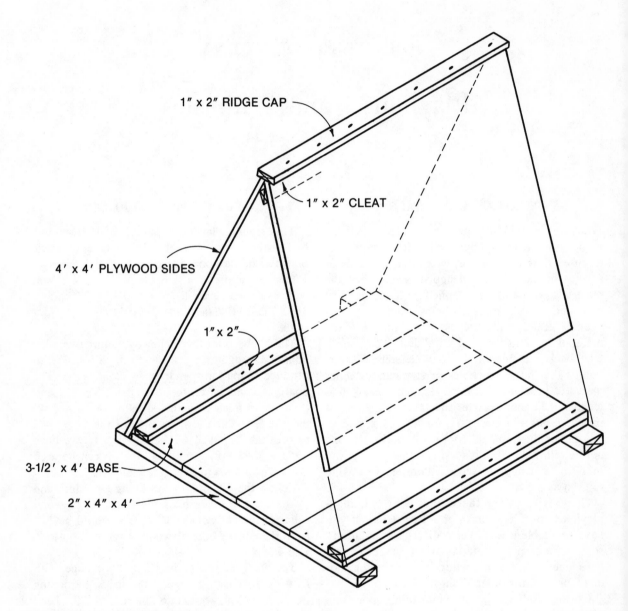

1″ x 2″ RIDGE CAP

1″ x 2″ CLEAT

4′ x 4′ PLYWOOD SIDES

1″ x 2″

3-1/2′ x 4′ BASE

2″ x 4″ x 4′

Fig. 105. **A-Frame Play Shelter, construction details.**

Then use 8d finishing nails to tie the shelter together along the ridgeline at the top. As a final finishing touch, run a line of caulk or other sealant along the ridgeline and nail a 4' length of 1" × 4" over it to close the cracks where the sides meet the ridgeboard. Painting is optional; or you might cover the sides with shingles or roll roofing.

SANDBOX SHELTER

In new subdivisions and in arid areas of the country where shade trees are scarce, sandboxes, wading pools, and other play areas for children often need larger shelters than can be provided by the small A-frame shelter just detailed.

There are several methods which can be used to construct a shelter, depending on the size desired. Larger shelters can be partly or completely decked; often a sandbox or wading pool can be centered in a deck under a large shelter to provide shade for adults, too.

The smallest and simplest of the shelters is one with an open slat roof supported by two central beams with the roof supports centered on the beams. A maximum area of about 10' × 10' can be covered by such a shelter.

Its construction is very simple. Set 6" × 6" posts of redwood or treated lumber in holes centered any desired distance up to 10' apart and filled with sack-mixed concrete. See Chapter Nine for the method of setting these posts. When the concrete has hardened, saw the posts off at a height of 6'6" from the ground and to their inside faces bolt 10' horizontal arms of 2" × 4"s, and brace the arms with diagonal 2" × 4"s which are also bolted to the center posts.

Cut slats of No. 3 common 1" × 4" or 1" × 6" lumber to fit between the arms. Beginning at the center post, set the slats extending to one end of the arms at a 45° angle to the arms, using a 3" to 4" spacing block to place them uniformly. Nail through the arms into the ends of the slats. On the other side of the shelter, set the slats at a 90° angle to the first slats (although they will still be at a 45° angle to the arms) out to the end of the supports. Nail center spacing blocks between the slats as they are set.

This type of shelter should be oriented to the sun, and the orientation will change depending on the latitude along which it is located. The orientation of the shelter's long side will be roughly north-south, which means that direct sunlight will shine through the slats during the morning and late afternoon hours. Ask the nearest National Weather Service meteorological observer to help you orient the shelter. These observers are stationed in small communities within 80 to 100 miles from the Weather Service's manned station.

To expand a shelter of this type, use corner posts rather than center posts, with a 4" × 4" beam across the tops of the posts. Spans up to 16' can be covered this way. For a longer span, use both corner posts and center posts.

PLAYHOUSE

A very satisfactory playhouse that will serve pre-teenagers can be made by using much the same technique used in building the A-frame shelter. Enlarge the dimensions of the foundation platform to 6' × 8', the size of one and a half plywood sheets. The remaining half sheet will be used to fill gable openings in the side walls. Preferably, ⅝" exterior-grade plywood should be used for floor and walls, though ¾" plywood can be safely substituted. The roof, fabricated by the same method given in the tent plan, can be of ⅜" plywood.

Begin by building the platform-foundation. This is made with 2" × 4" floor joists on edge, set on 24" centers. Use a 2" × 4" header along each side of the building. Preframe the walls and ends before erecting them. Use full sheets of plywood for the side walls, but reverse conventional building practice by placing the 1" × 4" sole and top plates and the 1" × 2" "studs" on the outsides of the walls. Nail and glue these to the wall sheets, with the edges of the plates flush with the plywood edges and the "studs" centered 24" between the plates.

Use a waterproof urea resin glue. No clamping will be required, as the nails will maintain the required contact between the glued surfaces. However, when the "rafters" are installed on the roof panels, as described in the preceding plan, these should be placed on the inside surfaces. The finished walls will give the playhouse the appearance of having board and batten exterior siding. Be sure, after assembling, to allow the glue to dry thoroughly before erecting the panels.

Erect the walls in the conventional manner, a side wall first, toenailed to the foundation. Use 16d box nails for this, and be sure that the

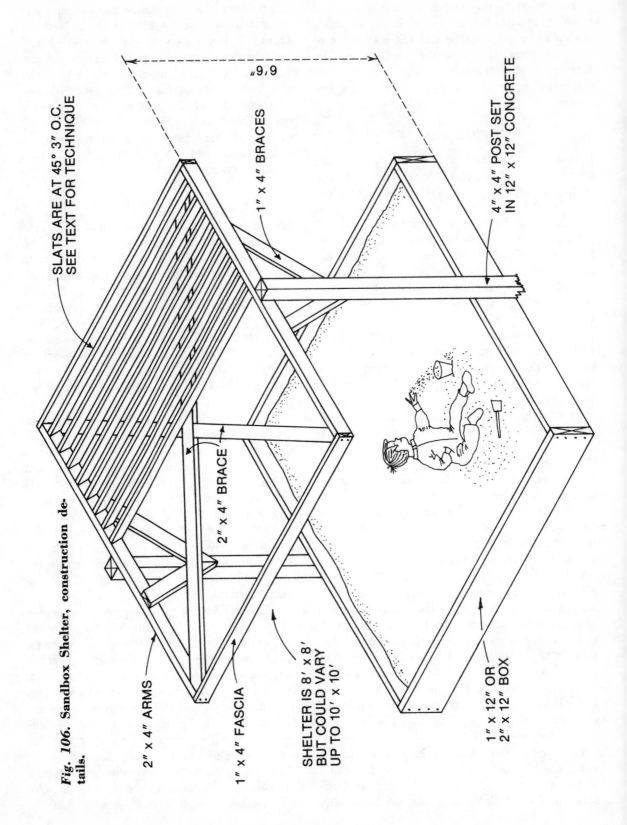

9' 9"

SLATS ARE AT 45° 3" O.C.
SEE TEXT FOR TECHNIQUE

1" x 4" BRACES

4" x 4" POST SET
IN 12" x 12" CONCRETE

2" x 4" BRACE

2" x 4" ARMS

1" x 4" FASCIA

SHELTER IS 8' x 8'
BUT COULD VARY
UP TO 10' x 10'

1" x 12" OR
2" x 12" BOX

Fig. 106. **Sandbox Shelter, construction details.**

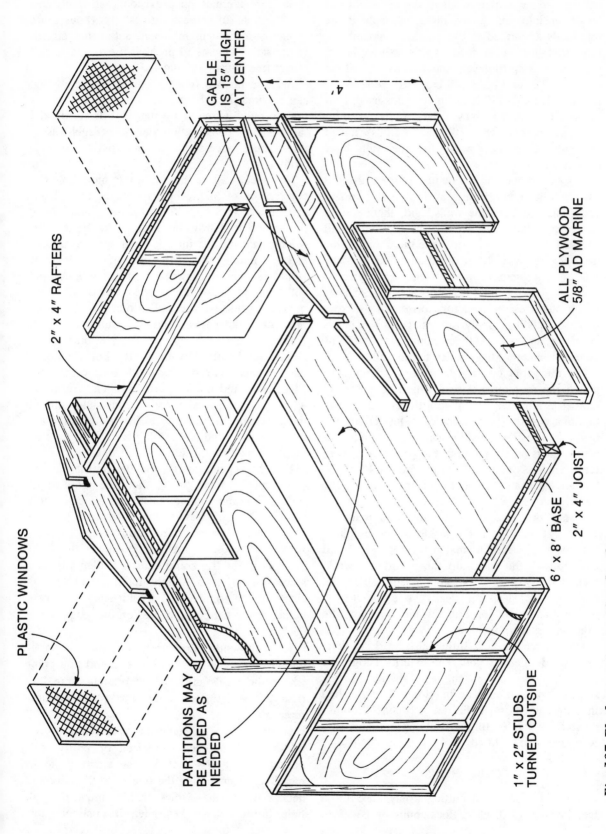

GABLE
IS 15" HIGH
AT CENTER

2" x 4" RAFTERS

ALL PLYWOOD
5/8" AD MARINE

2" x 4" JOIST

6' x 8' BASE

PLASTIC WINDOWS

PARTITIONS MAY
BE ADDED AS
NEEDED

1" x 2" STUDS
TURNED OUTSIDE

4'

Fig. 107. Playhouse, construction details.

nailing is done at points where the nails will not be driven into joist joints; these may split if the toed nails are added to those used in assembling the foundation. When the first side wall is placed, trued with a spirit level, and braced, install an end wall. The end walls will be 45½″ wide if ⅝″ plywood is used, 45″ if ¾″ plywood is used. Nail through the side wall into the end walls and reinforce the corners with 1″ × 2″ "studs" nailed and glued over the cracks after the walls have been placed.

Cut a door opening in one of the side walls and cut small window openings as desired in side and end walls. To keep the walls rigid, there should be no more than one window in each end wall and two in the side wall opposite the door. Frame the openings with 1″ × 2″ lumber on the outside. A door can be made from ⅜″ plywood. For safety, make windowpanes of acrylic. Sheets of various sizes are sold for storm sash windows at most building supply houses. Hold the panes in place and frame them with base shoe or quarter-round moldings nailed to the wall.

Fill the gable opening by cutting triangles to match the roof pitch. Use a length of 1″ × 6″ lumber as a batten, butting it at the corners to the top plates with the bottom edge leveled to the plates to provide a nailing surface. Use glue as well as nails on the edges of the walls and the interior surface of the batten, and add a 1″ × 2″ batten, glued and nailed to the inside along the joint.

Install two interior partition-braces made of 1″ × 12″ lumber in the inside of the building. Cut the upper ends to match the roof pitch and nail through the roof into the partition boards; toenail the boards to the floor inside. Space the partitions as desired; ideally, one should be within 14″ to 16″ on one side of the door, the other across from the door.

How much or how little finish work is done must be decided by you. The exterior should be painted; two coats on the roof should provide sufficient protection. The interior can be finished in different colors if desired to define "rooms" created by the partitions. Cabinets of ¼″ plywood can also be fitted.

TREE HOUSE

Before you set about putting a playhouse into a tree in your yard, check local building codes to make sure there is no provision that would bar construction. In some localities, tree houses are explicitly forbidden, in others authorities stretch vague safety clauses to prohibit them, and in still others tree houses are allowed.

Because no two trees are alike, about all that can be done here is to give you general ideas of how to build a tree house that will be sturdy and safe. Actual construction details of such structures must necessarily be improvised by the builder.

First, select a tree that has a minimum bole circumference of 50″, which translates to a diameter of 16″, at a point 6′ above the ground. Give preference to hardwood trees rather than softwoods. Hardwoods include such species as oak, hickory, maple, and in this case, pine; softwoods would take in cottonwood, cedar, hemlock, and willow. If you must use a softwood tree, the floor or deck should be installed so that it will be supported by branches as well as the trunk.

For decking supports, use 2″ × 8″ lumber attached to the trunk with 8″ lag bolts. Place a main support on each side of the tree, with upper edges level and the supports parallel. Use 2″ × 4″ or 2″ × 6″ lumber for decking, and support the decking at right angles to the trunk with diagonal braces bolted with 8″ lag bolts onto perimeter stringers on both sides of the trunk.

For the superstructure, use the fewest number of framing members possible and the lightest possible siding and roofing. In almost all cases, this means 2″ × 2″ framing members and ¼″ exterior-grade plywood siding and roofing.

Provide access through an opening in the decking next to the trunk and build a ladder with side pieces rather than simply nailing and bolting cleats to the trunk itself. Avoid using an access ladder that must be supported on one edge of the deck.

Keep the entire structure as compact as possible. Deck perimeters should not extend to a point where the tree's main lower branches are less than 2″ in diameter, roughly 6½″ in circumference.

Given a tree of sufficient size, build a tree house with the deck supported or partly supported by cables—not ropes—attached to a metal collar encircling the tree 6′ to 8′ above the deck. Attach the cables with clamps through holes in the collar to keep them from slipping lat-

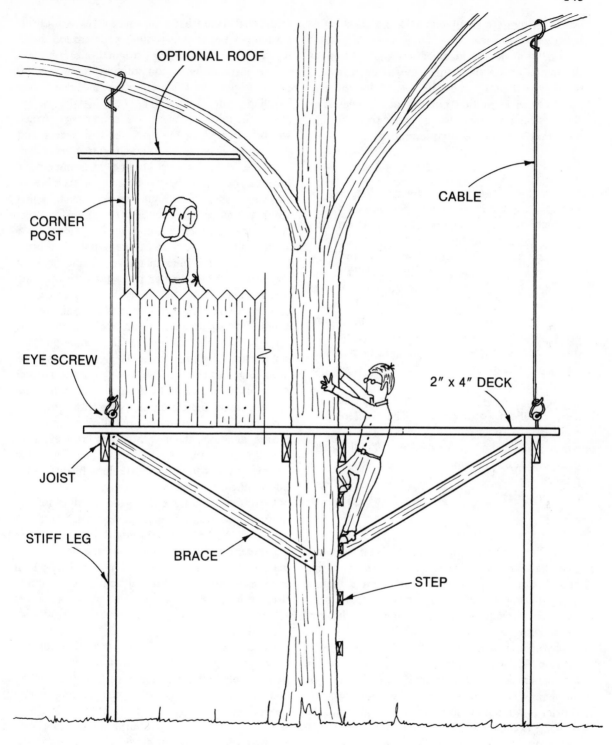

Fig. 108. Tree House, construction details.

erally. Aircraft control cable is the most satisfactory type to use.

Finally, avoid overloads of any kind: too many occupants at the same time, too much furniture, too many fittings. Don't be misled by the tree houses seen in motion pictures or on television; those structures are usually built on artificial trees that have a core of structural steel.

PERGOLA

A pergola, in case you're wondering, can be just about any type of small open garden shelter to which you want to apply the name. It can be a round, rectangular, square, or oval structure of any size and configuration, made from brick, laths, or lumber, with full or partial walls or side openings. It can have a flat, gabled, hip, gambrel, or pyramid-shaped roof. Any additional features you wish, such as bench seats, a fountain, a miniature waterfall, an old-fashioned lever-operated pump, can be added in the building or beside it. Let your imagination have full play when you plan your pergola.

Use the type of construction given in Chapter Ten in building your pergola. The chief requirement of a pergola is that it be small in size, accommodating at most four people. Traditionally, climbing roses or other vine-type growth was planted around the perimeter of a pergola to cover its sides.

GAZEBO

Unlike pergolas, this pre-Victorian whimsy does have a traditional shape. A gazebo should be either round or octagonal, and should feature a cupola atop a multisided gabled roof, the sides of the roof rising in the same planes as those of the building.

If you want a round gazebo, it's a simple matter to build one, using the same plan as that given for an octagonal structure and rounding off the corners. The corner floor joists must be cut shorter and the intermediate joists longer, and the decking boards must be sawed into arcs with a saber saw, if you elect to build in circular form.

Traditionally, gazebos are located in the center of a garden and on a small rise, artificial or natural, and are provided with a solid floor. Their original purpose was to provide a shelter for afternoon tea, so that the tea and a view of the garden could be enjoyed simultaneously. If you're a

traditionalist and have no garden, leave room at least for a flower bed around your gazebo as an indication of the building's original purpose.

Use post-and-beam construction, for which details are given in Chapters Nine and Ten, when building your gazebo. The only detail not included in those chapters is a center pier, which will be required for the gazebo's floor beams, and this will be given in the following paragraphs.

Set the eight corner posts first. Determine their location by using batter boards as detailed in Chapter Three to lay out two squares of equal size superimposed on one another at a 45° angle. A post is set in each corner of each square.

Determine the center of the foundation posts by running chalk lines in a straight line between any two of the perimeter posts that are opposite one another. Repeat. Where the lines cross, locate the center foundation pier. Pour this pier in a hole 24" square, setting an anchor bolt in the center. When the concrete of the center pier has set, anchor lengths of 4" × 4" along each side as a nailing surface for the floor beams. Toenail 4" × 4" floor beams to the perimeter posts and spike them to the center supports with 20d common nails driven through predrilled holes in the beams, or attach them with 6" lag bolts countersunk in the beams. Nail 2" × 4" braces to the perimeter posts to support the floor beams or reinforce them with metal T-plates.

Use redwood tongue and groove siding for the floor. If you want to economize a bit, use 1" × 10" or 1" × 12" redwood boards. Lay the flooring to center lines established on the floor beams with a chalk line. Because the angle at which each floorboard is sawed will be the same, simply use the first board cut as a pattern to mark the others. Nail the flooring in place with 8d corrugated shank nails.

Build courses of studding for the half walls just as you would build the stud assemblies for full-height walls, but use a single top plate. Cover the studding with redwood lap siding or tongue and groove siding or board and batten siding, and nail 1" × 6" redwood boards on the top plate between the posts as finish.

Install a top plate of 4" × 4" or 2" × 6" redwood to support the rafters; if 2" × 6" is used, it should be set on edge in notches cut in the supporting posts. Cut rafters of 2" × 6" redwood and saw a hexagonal collar of doubled ¾" exterior-grade plywood to which the upper ends of the rafters can be nailed. Notch the upper ends to accommodate the plate.

Make the cupola of ¾″ exterior-grade red-wood-faced plywood and toenail it to the collar.

Arched trim for the upper portion of the gazebo is made from 1½″ redwood lath.

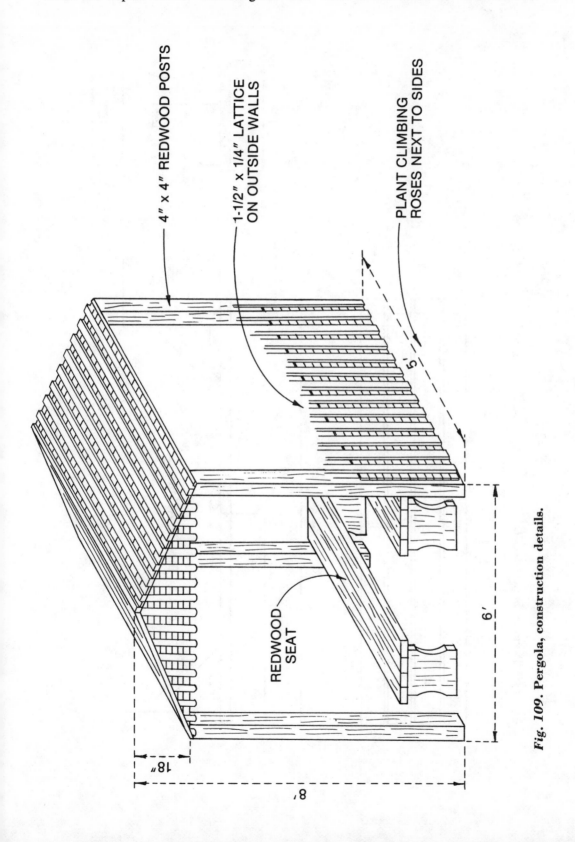

Fig. 109. Pergola, construction details.

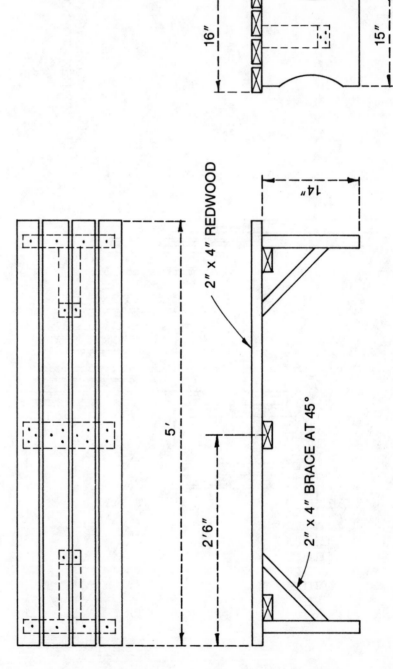

Fig. 110. Pergola, bench detail.

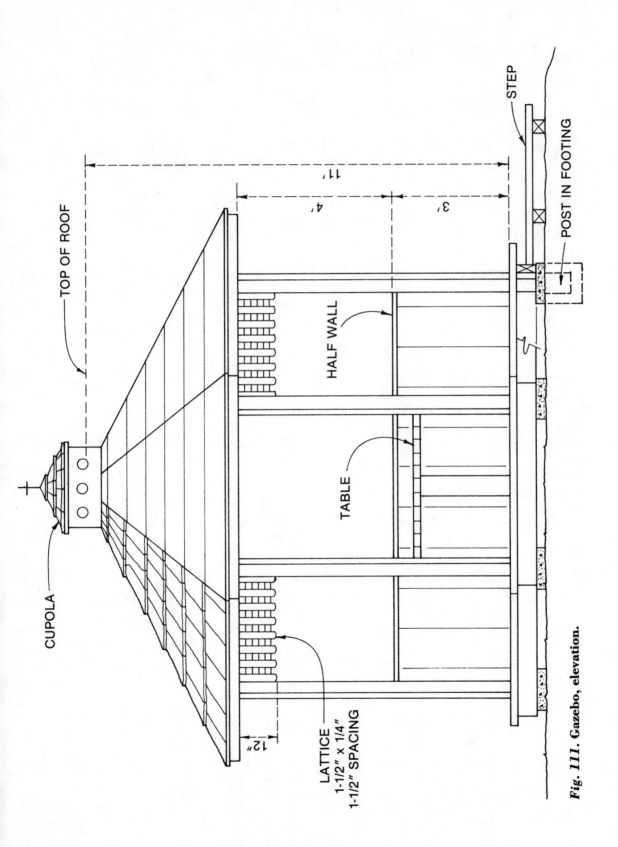

TOP OF ROOF

CUPOLA

LATTICE
1-1/2" x 1/4"
1-1/2" SPACING

12"

HALF WALL

TABLE

11'

4'

3'

STEP

POST IN FOOTING

Fig. 111. Gazebo, elevation.

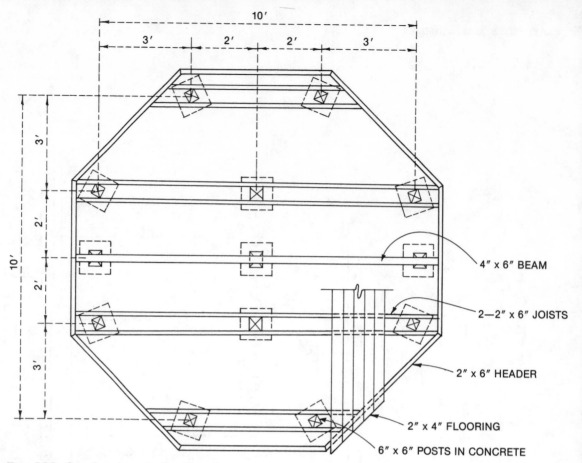

Fig. 112. Gazebo, foundation details.

- 4″ x 6″ BEAM
- 2—2″ x 6″ JOISTS
- 2″ x 6″ HEADER
- 2″ x 4″ FLOORING
- 6″ x 6″ POSTS IN CONCRETE

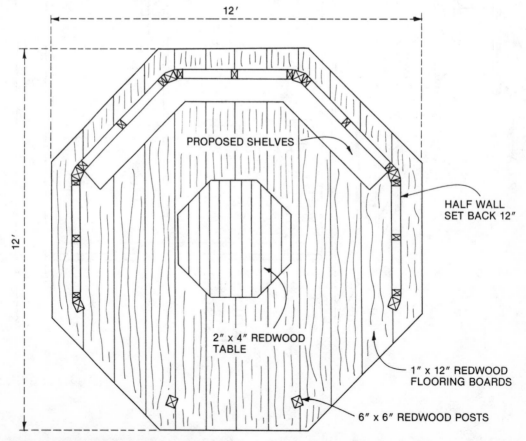

Fig. 113. Gazebo, floor plan.

- PROPOSED SHELVES
- HALF WALL SET BACK 12″
- 2″ x 4″ REDWOOD TABLE
- 1″ x 12″ REDWOOD FLOORING BOARDS
- 6″ x 6″ REDWOOD POSTS

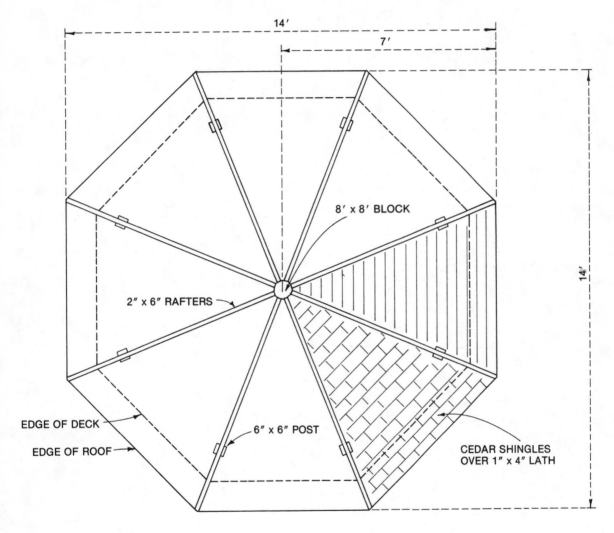

14'

7'

14'

8' x 8' BLOCK

2" x 6" RAFTERS

EDGE OF DECK

EDGE OF ROOF

6" x 6" POST

CEDAR SHINGLES
OVER 1" x 4" LATH

Fig. 114. **Gazebo, roof plan.**

Appendix A

AMERICAN STANDARD SOFTWOOD LUMBER DIMENSIONS

	THICKNESS			FACE WIDTH		
	Nominal	Dry	Green	Nominal	Dry	Green
	inches	inches	inches	inches	inches	inches
BOARDS	1	¾	$2\frac{5}{32}$	2	$1\frac{1}{2}$	$1\frac{9}{16}$
AND	$1\frac{1}{4}$	1	$1\frac{1}{32}$	3	$2\frac{1}{2}$	$2\frac{9}{16}$
STRIPS	$1\frac{1}{2}$	$1\frac{1}{4}$	$1\frac{9}{32}$	4	$3\frac{1}{2}$	$3\frac{9}{16}$
				5	$4\frac{1}{2}$	$4\frac{5}{8}$
				6	$5\frac{1}{2}$	$5\frac{5}{8}$
				7	$6\frac{1}{2}$	$6\frac{5}{8}$
				8	$7\frac{1}{4}$	$7\frac{1}{2}$
				9	$8\frac{1}{4}$	$8\frac{1}{2}$
				10	$9\frac{1}{4}$	$9\frac{1}{2}$
				11	$10\frac{1}{4}$	$10\frac{1}{2}$
				12	$11\frac{1}{4}$	$11\frac{1}{2}$
				14	$13\frac{1}{4}$	$13\frac{1}{2}$
				16	$15\frac{1}{4}$	$15\frac{1}{2}$
DIMENSION	2	$1\frac{1}{2}$	$1\frac{9}{16}$	2	$1\frac{1}{2}$	$1\frac{9}{16}$
LUMBER	$2\frac{1}{2}$	2	$2\frac{1}{16}$	3	$2\frac{1}{2}$	$2\frac{9}{16}$
	3	$2\frac{1}{2}$	$2\frac{9}{16}$	4	$3\frac{1}{2}$	$3\frac{9}{16}$
	$3\frac{1}{2}$	3	$3\frac{1}{16}$	5	$4\frac{1}{2}$	$4\frac{5}{8}$
	4	$3\frac{1}{2}$	$3\frac{9}{16}$	6	$5\frac{1}{2}$	$5\frac{5}{8}$
	$4\frac{1}{2}$	4	$4\frac{1}{16}$	8	$7\frac{1}{4}$	$7\frac{1}{2}$
				10	$9\frac{1}{4}$	$9\frac{1}{2}$
				12	$11\frac{1}{4}$	$11\frac{1}{2}$
				14	$13\frac{1}{4}$	$13\frac{1}{2}$
				16	$15\frac{1}{4}$	$15\frac{1}{2}$
TIMBERS	5 and greater		½″ less than nominal	5 and greater		½″ less than nominal

Example of use: You order 2″ × 4″ dimension lumber (nominal dimension). You get the "dry" or "green" thickness and face widths shown in those columns. A 2″ × 4″ from a lumber yard is 1½″ × 3½″.

ESTIMATED BOARD COVERAGE

Type	Nominal Dimension	Exposed Face	Coverage Factor in Board Feet
	inches	inches	
S4S	1 × 4	3½	1.14
	1 × 6	5½	1.10
	1 × 8	7½	1.09
	1 × 10	9¼	1.08
	1 × 12	11¼	1.07
Shiplap	1 × 6	5⅛	1.17
	1 × 8	6⅞	1.16
	1 × 10	8⅞	1.13
	1 × 12	10⅞	1.10
Tongue & Groove	1 × 4	3⅛	1.28
	1 × 6	5⅛	1.17
	1 × 8	6⅞	1.16
	1 × 10	9¼	1.13
	1 × 12	10⅞	1.10
Bevel Siding	1 × 6	5½	1.33
	1 × 8	7¼	1.28
	1 × 10	9¼	1.21
	1 × 12	11¼	1.17
Lap Siding	1 × 6	4½	1.46
	1 × 6	5	1.32
	1 × 9	7¼	1.26
	1 × 9	8	1.185
	1 × 12	10½	1.20
	1 × 12	10	1.15

To use the tables above, first multiply the *surface areas* of all exterior wall to be covered, to determine the number of *square feet* of lumber required. Then, multiply the number of *square feet* by the *coverage factor* in the right-hand column to find the number of *board feet* of the width lumber you plan to use.

Remember that *board feet* is a measurement of *volume* and *square feet* is a measurement of *area*. When using any lapped pattern lumber, such as shiplap or tongue and groove, the volume of lumber that goes into the overlaps must be taken into account. The only types of lumber in which the edges butt together without overlapping are S4S (surfaced four sides) and S2E (surfaced two edges).

Appendix B

NAIL SIZE CHART

COMMON NAILS (A)

Size	Length	Approx. Number Per Pound
5d	2″	192
6d	2″	181
7d	2¼″	163
8d	2½″	106
9d	2½″	92
10d	3″	69
12d	3¼″	63
16d	3½″	49
20d	4″	31

FINISHING NAILS (D)

Size	Length	Approx. Number Per Pound
6d	2″	309
8d	2½″	189
10d	3″	121
16d	3½″	90

CASING NAILS (E)

Size	Length	Approx. Number Per Pound
6d	2″	236
8d	2½″	145
10d	3½″	71

ROOFING NAILS (B)*		PLASTERBOARD NAILS (C)*	
Length	Approx. Number Per Pound	Length	Approx. Number Per Pound
¾"	315	1¼"	425
1"	255	1½"	319
1¼"	210		
1½"	180		
2"	138		

* Roofing and plasterboard nails are sized by their length only.

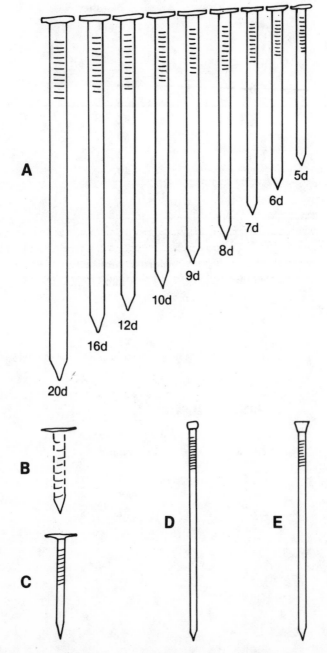

—*Chart courtesy C F & I*